IN THE LAND OF CHILDHOOD

HEBREW CHILDREN'S LITERATURE

IN THE LAND OF CHILDHOOD

HEBREW CHILDREN'S LITERATURE

YAIR MAZOR

HenschelHAUS Publishing, Inc.
Milwaukee, Wisconsin

Published by
HenschelHAUS Publishing, Inc.
www.henschelHAUSbooks.com

ISBN: 978159598-819-5
E-ISBN:978159598-820-1
LCCN: 2020952907

For my beloved niece, Attorney Chamutal K. Beno, whose
incredibly paramount help, love, and devotion,
made this book possible .

And for my beloved parents, Rachel and Yitzchak ,
Who have left the land of the living
But never my heart.

~ ~ ~ ~ ~

"We think our fathers fools, so wise we grow.
Our wiser sons, no doubt will think us so."
—Alexander Pope, *Essay on Criticism*, Part 2,
line 238)

"The child is father of the man."
—William Wordsworth,
"My Heart Leaps up When I Behold"

CONTENTS

Who's Afraid of Hebrew Children's Literature, and Why?
Or: The Importance of Being Earnest about Cinderella

"She taught the child to read, and taught so well,
That she herself, by teaching, learn'd to spell."
—Byron, "Sketch"

The earliest known written literary text that primarily addresses children is probably the ancient Egyptian papyrus, The *Laws of Ptkh-Khtp* (2600 BCE), which includes moral fables for the "good son." However, the development of Western children's literature did not gather momentum until the end of the seventeenth century. A landmark in children's literature is Charles Perrault's Contes de ma Mere l'Oye (1697), including the well-known story, *Little Red Riding Hood.*

The history of critical writing about children's literature is even shorter, probably beginning around 1918, the year Anne Carol Morre published her literary study of Henry Hudson's *A Little Boy Lost.* (1)

It is well known that children's literature, as well as its writers, have suffered from poor self-image, for historical, social, and literary reasons. One reason may be that literary criticism aimed at children's literature has been primarily directed at the educational and psychological aspects of the works. At times it seems as if the critics almost apologetically took this route in order to prove the merits of children's literature, despite its perceived limited poetic value. In light of this, the following statement by Zohar Shavit is particularly apt. "I believe the time has come to extricate children's literature from the narrow boundaries of the past and to replace it in the literary scholarship facing the future." (2)

Indeed, the various differences between children and adults, including degrees of intellectual faculty, cognitive capacity, emotional maturity, and command of language dictate different standards of literary decorum for children's literature and, correspondingly, different critical considerations. As James Steel Smith put it: "The criteria relevant to adult literature and the criteria relevant to children's literature may differ markedly in important ways." (3) Nevertheless, the critical attitude toward children's literature should share a common denominator with the attitude toward literature in general. According to Paul Heins, "A children's book deserves to be probed as much as an adult book for general questions of diction, structure, significance of detail, and literary integrity." (4)

Despite such useful statements, however, the following observation by Lillian H. Smith still seems regretfully valid. "There are those who think of a children's book as just a simpler treatment of an adult theme. This point of view considers children as only diminutive adults and arises from a misunderstanding of childhood itself."

Children's literature is literature, a legitimate and equal literary system within the comprehensive system of literature, a worthy literary body that deserves aesthetic appreciation as well as scholarly recognition. Although children's literature at the dawn of its evolution was adopted, cultivated, and monitored by the educational establishment, it is not an educational form. Children's literature, like all literature, displays a historical-literary evolution that is affected by such nonliterary factors as culture and society, the dynamic between the mainstream and the margins, modes and genres, and canonized and non-canonized literary works.

The development of Hebrew children's literature resembles the evolution of non-Hebrew Western children's literature in two ways: it began evolving quite late, at the end of the nineteenth century, and it was similarly engaged with educational systems. The late evolution of Hebrew children's literature (in Europe) was naturally conditioned by the late development of *Haskalah* ("Enlightenment") literature (1780-1870). Modern *Haskalah* literature (Hebrew secular literature) was initiated and propelled by ideological, educational values—in particular, the wish to demolish the limiting walls of the Jewish mental ghetto in Europe and to encourage Jews to add secular education to their Talmudic-religious education.

It is natural, then, that *Haskalah* children's literature would convey educational values and attitudes. However, despite the fact that the emergence of a new Hebrew secular literature in the *Haskalah* period initiated and influenced children's literature, the emergence of Hebrew children's literature did not occur before *Haskalah* literature reached its peak. This lag may be attributed to the fact that the *Maskilim* (*Haskalah* ideologues and activists) encountered extreme resistance from the orthodox Jewish leaders who resented their deviation from religious education and their pursuit of secular education. Consequently, the Maskilim invested all their energy in advocating and carrying out their principle philosophy; thus, the investment in children's literature was not a top priority. Nevertheless, the establishment of the first Jewish day schools in Europe eventually yielded the first Hebrew books for children.

Hebrew textbooks for children were published at the beginning of the *Haskalah* period. These works include: Avtalyon, by A. Wolfson-Halleh (Berlin, 1770) and Bet-Sefer: *Messilat Halimud* ("School: A Teaching Track"), by Y. L. Ben-Ze'ev (Berlin, 1802), which includes the first Hebrew poems written for children. These first Hebrew volumes for children are characteristically educational, and their prime purpose is pedagogic-tutorial, not aesthetic.

The first volumes for children, which primarily had an aesthetic and entertaining purpose, were the following anthologies of Hebrew stories: "Tal Yaldut" ("Childhood's Dew") by Sh. Ziskind Rashkov (Bratislava, 1834), and "Mikveh Israel" ("Israel's Collection/Pool") by I. Costa (Livorno, 1851). During the second half of the nineteenth century, David Zamosc of Bratislava was one of the most prolific Hebrew writers for children; he published about twenty Hebrew children's volumes.

However, the most famous Hebrew writer for children has traditionally been Abraham Mapu (Russia, 1808-1867), the creator of the first Hebrew novel, *Ahavat Tzion* ("Love of Zion," 1853). In 1867, Mapu published a tutorial volume for teaching Hebrew, *Amon Pedagog* ("A Master Pedagogue"), that included a short story entitled, *Bet*

Hanan ("The House of Hanan"). *Bet Hanan* inspired numerous works of children's literature—originals, translations, and adaptations of works from foreign languages. Many of these books have educational-Zionist qualities, inspired by the rise of Hebrew nationalism in Europe and the establishment of the Zionist movement. The anthology of children's stories, *Sikhot Mini Kedem* ("Tales of Ancient Days"), by S. Jabez (Warsaw, 1887), is considered an aesthetic milestone in the evolution of Hebrew children's literature. Mapu set an example for later celebrated Hebrew writers who published works for children, mostly during the 1920s and 1940s. Among those writers were the poets Chaim Nachman Bialik, Jacob Fichman, Zalman Shneur, and Itzhak Katzenelson.

Since the second decade of the twentieth century, the center of modern Hebrew literature gradually shifted from Eastern Europe to the Land of Israel. However, the first Hebrew children's volume was published in the Land of Israel prior to the end of the nineteenth century. In 1878, Eliezer Ben-Yehuda (1858-1922), the celebrated reviver of Hebrew as a modern spoken language, and the compiler of the first modern Hebrew dictionary, together with Hebrew scholar and educator David Levin, published the first Hebrew children's book, *A Reader for Israel's Children*.

During the 1920s, one of the most celebrated Hebrew writers for children in the Land of Israel was Levin Kipnis. Other prominent Hebrew writers for children between the 1920s and 1940s were Nachum Gutman, who was also a prominent painter, Yakov Churgin, Yemima Tchernovitz, and Eliezer Smoli, who wrote children's stories about

Hebrew guards and pioneers in the period prior to statehood.

The challenging, yet glorious, days of establishing the old-new Jewish homeland in Palestine provided a realistic background for many of the children's literary works. The aesthetic style of those works was primarily lyrical and romantic, and the plots combined realism with imagination. Since the early 1940s, the most distinguished children's storytellers were Leah Goldberg, who was also a remarkable poet, playwright, translator, and professor of comparative literature; Anda Amir-Pinkerfeld; and Miriam Yalan-Stekelis.

Miriam Yalan-Stekelis (1900-1989) was one of those singular children's poets whose aesthetics and psychological attitude toward her young readers always displayed great affection and respect. Significantly, Yalan-Stekelis's literary works for children never addressed the child from an Olympic pedestal that projects adult superiority over the child. Rather, her works address the child as a young person whose conceptual world and intellectual faculties deserve the most serious and respectful consideration. The fact that many of Yalan-Stekelis's children's poems express subtle sadness, and even a tinge of gloom, while deliberately avoiding a rosy, overly sweet and unrealistic approach to life, is an aesthetic indication of her serious and respectful attitude toward her young readers. Her poems for children neither attempt to deceive the child (from a patronizing adult viewpoint) nor to sell the child a fictional world that is incongruent with the state of the real world.

Such a serious and respectful aesthetic-psychological approach to children's literature, which prefers honest sincerity to patronizing falsehood, is also evident in the literary works that the distinguished poet Saul Tchernichovsky (1875-1943) wrote for children (see "Snow White Does Not Live Here Anymore," in my book on Tchernichovsky's narrative art, *The Other Tchernichovsky: His Narrative Landscape* [Tel Aviv: Papyrus, Tel Aviv University, 1992] pp. 161-176.)

Other well-known Israeli poets who wrote poems for children were Abraham Shlonsky (1900-1973) and Nathan Alterman (1910-1970). Shlonsky and Alterman's children's poetry is distinguished for its sharp, witty verbal acrobatics, its puns and rhymes. Their children's poetry never lowers its aesthetic standards, but rather demonstrates an underlying aesthetic, educational purpose: to challenge its young audience intellectually.

Among the most distinguished Israeli novelists and storytellers who have written for children—mostly since the 1960s—are S. Yizhar [Smilansky] (1916-2006), Moshe Shamir (1921-2004), Nathan Shaham (b. 1925), and Benjamin Tamuz (1919-1989). A well-known Israeli series of adventure novels for children, called *Hassamba* (acronym for "most secret group") by Yigal Mossinson, was first published in the 1950s and has been enjoying tremendous success ever since. Although the *Hassamba* novels do not possess much aesthetic value, and their fictional world is over-simplified, they advocate positive educational values such as initiative, creativity, friendship, originality, loyalty, and responsibility.

Uriel Ofek was, for several decades, a respected and prolific leading figure in modern Israeli children's literature. Ofek was not only a writer of children's literature, but a very active editor of the well-known children's periodical *Davar Liladim* ("Children's Word"). He was also a highly knowledgeable scholar of children's literature. Ofek dedicated his doctoral dissertation to Hebrew children's literature and produced numerous scholarly volumes on that subject, including a detailed encyclopedia of Hebrew and world children's literature.

Many contemporary Israeli writers continue Mapu's laudable tradition of writing children's literature. Among them are: David Grossman (b. 1954), Amos Oz (b. 1939), Meir Shalev (b. 1948), and the poet Dalia Rabikovitz (1936–2004). Among the most visible contemporary Israeli children's writers are Yehuda Atlas, Jonathan Geffen, and Nurit Zarhi. Quite recently, however, the celebrated poet Ronny Someck published a children's book, jointly composed with his seven-year-old daughter, Shirley.

Hebrew children's literature has never been so thriving and prosperous as it is nowadays. In this respect, the question "Who's afraid of Hebrew children's literature, and why?" may seem nothing but a shallow cliché. It depends, of course, on what one means by the word "afraid." If the word is associated with concern or reservation, then the question may have some validity. The inquiry may be extended beyond the national poetic boundaries of Hebrew children's literature. Who could find any children's literature threatening? Isn't children's literature the most innocent and harmless type of literature? It is far from being so.

Bruno Bettelheim, in his celebrated study (5) examines the underlying currents of seemingly innocent and harmless children's fairy tales and legends. Bettelheim argues that the plots of such apparently naïve fairy tales, which seem enticing and sweet, in fact cunningly conceal cryptic meanings loaded with emotions such as fear, anxiety, and danger.

Once one gets beneath the surface of children's literature and its cryptic message, one can understand more clearly the power of these texts and why some might fear it. This is especially true when the literature is associated with education.

Traditionally, there has been a connection between children's literature and education. When the genre started gaining momentum in Europe in the eighteenth century, it was largely monopolized by religious educators. As was the case with theater in the Middle Ages, the European church controlled the writing and the distribution of children's literature. It shaped those texts to reflect its religious teaching.

There is another element associated with education. Although the attitude of society toward children has progressed dramatically since the eighteenth century, there is still a tendency to underestimate a child's intellectual capability. Historically, children's literature has been underestimated aesthetically. It has not been considered part of *belles lettres*, but rather an instrument, a vehicle used for delivering an educational message to children.

Indeed, both the historical attitude toward children as undeveloped, deficient adults, and consequently, the traditional view of children's literature as a vehicle to convey an educational message, contribute to the lowly position of children's literature as an aesthetic creation. At the same time, however, its educational power has been recognized and feared. Those who traditionally are wary of ideas and education are easily persuaded to fear what they perceive as an educational tool, especially if it is in the hands of those who have different beliefs and values.

As stated earlier, it is certainly time to treat children's literature, while different from adult literature, as a valuable and important literary genre that has distinct aesthetic merit. The educational aspects of children's literature do not reduce its aesthetic value. Since children's literature has traditionally been viewed as an educational means, it is closely scrutinized by those who fear education. And when it comes to Hebrew children's literature, and to its presumed educational tendencies, the matter does not become any simpler.

The most impressive body of children's literature began to gain ground in the early decades of the twentieth century at the time that the first wave of Zionists returned to the Land of Israel (Palestine), which parallels a revival of the Hebrew language. A rather simplified, but no less valid, portrayal of the emotional, intellectual, historical, and social atmosphere during the Zionist pioneering days addresses two concerns. On the one hand, the return from the Jewish diaspora to the old-new homeland, the land of the glorious Jewish-Biblical past, inspired the newcomers to shape and foster a new type of Jew, a Jew freed from what was perceived as the diaspora Jew's submissiveness, meekness, physical weakness, and spiritual humility. Hence, the Zionist fervent dream was to create and shape a new type of Jew who is physically strong and assertive, mighty, and daring; a Jew deeply rooted in his homeland, willing and capable of defending it; a Jew possessing the might and the courage of historical figures, such as King David and King Solomon, or the venerable hero Bar-Kokhba (the legendary leader of the rebellion against the Romans in 132 CE).

Certainly, the national recollection of the atrocities of the Holocaust, in which more than six million Jews were exterminated by the Nazis, further fueled the desire to mold Jews who bravely take their fate in their own hands and assertively respond to any national challenge. Also, the decades-long bloody conflict with Israel's Arab neighbors strengthened the wish of Israelis to adopt ideals of military might, courage, and confidence. Thus, blatant national determination inspired by slogans such as "no more pogroms," "no more persecution," and "no more Holocaust," encouraged Israelis to replace the lamb with the lion in their national portrait. In this respect, the new Israelis consciously chose to be both David and Goliath, while replacing the previous submissiveness with furious assertiveness.

However, the new Israelis have never felt totally comfortable with forsaking traditional Jewish values, such as humanism, patient tolerance, and intellectual scholarship. This national self-image, with its conflicting attributes, produces psychological confusion. The obstinate wish to marry Kind David's might and Samson's aggressiveness with the humane, compassionate, and peaceful prophecies of Isaiah and Jeremiah inevitably leads to a self-contradiction that is reflected in the symbol of the *Sabra*

(*Tzabar*), which is applied to native-born Israelis. The Sabra is a cactus that is thorny and rough on the surface yet sweet and mellow on the inside. The symbol of the Sabra is, therefore, not only a national statement on the part of the new Israelis, but also an educational model and a message that they want to deliver to new Israeli generations, Therefore, this conflicting dual national image emerges in many works of modern Hebrew children's literature.

Thus, parents who are not comfortable with the assertive aspect of the message, parents who are not comfortable with the submissive aspect of the message, or parents who are not comfortable with the contradictions of the message, may also be uncomfortable with this kind of children's literature. I refer to parents because, in general, parents are the ones buying children's books, reading them, or monitoring their children's reading.

The contradictory Sabra message in Hebrew children's literature is only one component in a large and complex network of topics, themes, issues, and motifs. Moreover, the Sabra message is not as widespread in contemporary Hebrew children's literature as it was a few decades ago, when Israel's struggle for existence and independence was at its height. Still, the message is part of that literature and has never been entirely banished from the collective Israeli consciousness.

Neither the aesthetic, educational-psychological content of children's literature nor its special audience should diminish the poetic virtues of this literary genre. It should not be regarded as a "step-child" of other types of literature, but rather as a unique genre of its own. Literature is literature is literature. And children's literature is a legitimate subject for literary criticism. The importance of being earnest about Cinderella should be beyond any doubt. Indeed, the uniqueness of this literary genre, which primarily addresses young readers whose conceptual thinking, life experience, and vocabulary are unique, dictates a fresh scholarly approach. The scholarly approach, then, should be congruent with the genre.

The poor critical/scholarly perception of children's literature is not the only difficulty a writer of such literature must confront. The unique genre features an aesthetic complexity that is different from the concerns of the writer of adult literature. Accordingly, the children's writer is the only one who is expected and, indeed, compelled to address, satisfy, and appeal to two dramatically different types of readers.

On the one hand, the child is the official "implied reader" of children's literature, its natural and targeted audience. On the other hand, the adult who either purchases the work on the child's behalf, or reads it to the child (or guides the child's reading), the unofficial "implied reader" is also being addressed. The gulf between children and adults (conceptual comprehension, life experience, literary-cultural background, command of vocabulary, principal approach to reality, etc.) forces aesthetic and intellectual constraints on the writer. As Zohar Shavit put it, "Writers find various solutions to this problem, the most extreme being ignoring one of the addressees. Either the child is used as a mere excuse, or the adult reader is ignored, which may risk his/her rejection." (6)

However, most writers for children do not try to bypass these constraints but rather accept them as a framework for handling the problem of their specific genre. Correspondingly, those writers who address both children and adults simultaneously are forced to make a compromise between two conflicting styles of writing. Shavit maintains that this compromise is achieved by employing strategies of "compensation," while remaining within the limits of the prevailing norms of the system, in order to reach both kinds of reader. (7)

While children's literature, which primarily approaches the child while ignoring the adult, tends to end up as non-canonized literature, children's literature that prefers the adult over the child tends to encourage ambivalence. The ambivalent text maintains a simplified surface model that addresses the child and a latent, complicated and challenging model that addresses the adult, sometimes while making a parody of the surface model. Only an adult reader has the ability to fully understand the text and to relate to both models, as well as to the ironic tension that exists between the two. The child, whose capacity for textual realization is limited, is left with the surface, more simplified model.

Usually, the two different tracks, or levels, which the writer establishes and cultivates, display a reciprocal congruency. Accordingly, the upper level of the text (the epidermic, surface layer), which communicates with the child (the official audience), conveys a certain message in a rather simplified manner. The internal, latent layer of the text, which communicates with the adult (implied reader), delivers a similar message, but with an aesthetic complexity that satisfies the adult's developed intellectual faculties.

Thus, while the two layers of the text's message are principally the same, they differ aesthetically in order to satisfy these two different types of reader. It may happen, though, that the gap between the two layers of the text goes beyond the dosage of aesthetic intricacy and intellectual complexity. In such cases, the two conveyed messages of the text do not differ only in aesthetic and intellectual intricacy, but they also differ on an ideological level. Thus, the children's text delivers one ideological message to the child while addressing the adult reader with a drastically different ideological message.

Such cases are likely to be related to the confusing Sabra message, which has been internalized by Israeli society. The underlying educational values absorbed and demonstrated by the children's literature, as well as the prevailing perception of it as an effective educational instrument, make children's literature not only a means of social-ideological communication, but also a social barometer that measures, displays, and conveys the ideological credo and set of values of the society.

Since the contradictory image of the Sabra is part of the value system of Israeli society (although it has significantly decreased during the last two or three decades), it is very likely to filter into children's literature. The Sabra image, with its combination of assertiveness and sensitivity, is a natural element in children's literature, bridging the gap between the epidermic layer (aiming at the child) and the latent layer (aiming at the adult).

The poem "Danny Gibor" ("Danny the Hero"), by Miriam Yalan-Stekelis, can serve as a case study that shows how conflicting values are both absorbed and reflected by that most sensitive seismograph, children's literature. The poem is a successful example of Zohar Shavit's ambivalent model. Miriam Yalan-Stekelis makes a clever use of the ambivalent model. While cultivating a complex stratum of poetics that can be appreciated by a discerning adult reader, the poem does not abandon its official implied reader, the child.

The layer of the poem that addresses the child may be called the surface or "epidermic" layer. The layer of the poem that addresses the adult, however, may be called the internal or latent layer. Thus, the poem can be discussed in terms of its stratified structure of two layers: the upper layer addresses the child, while the deep structure (a term borrowed from Noam Chomsky's generative-transformative grammar) addresses the adult. The deep structure of the poem in its turn, also has two layers: the latent layer, and hidden beneath it, the cryptic layer. That cryptic layer is based on a Biblical allusion to Samson (*Judges 13-15*). Moreover, the cryptic allusive layer and the latent layer are bound by an analogy. Thus, the poem holds three layers: surface layer, latent layer, and cryptic-allusive layer.

The surface layer, which is anchored in the poem's upper structure, addresses the child, while the latent and the cryptic-allusive layers, which form the poem's deep structure, addresses the adult. However, the poem's stratified structure is even more intricate. The two layers of the deep structure display a tight analogy that drastically contradicts the upper structure of the poem by dint of both rhetoric and ideas. The message delivered to the child by the upper structure is in dramatic conflict with the message conveyed to the adult through the deep structure. The reciprocal relationship between the upper and deep structure of the poem might be called an oxymoron: one unit containing simultaneously two contradictory components. Thus, the poem is a prime example of the ambivalent model. The following close reading of the poem aims to demonstrate this point.

The Testing Task of Being a Hero
—The Poem "Danny the Hero"
by Miriam Yalan-Stekelis

Danny the Hero (Danny Gibor) (8)

Mother said to me—Danny
My child is a hero and clever.
My child will never cry
Like a little fool.

I do not ever cry,
I am not a crybaby.
It is just the tears... the tears they
Cry by themselves.

I gave Nurit a flower,
A little one, pretty and blue.
I gave Nurit an apple
I gave everything.

Nurit ate the apple,
She threw the flower in the yard,
She went to play with a boy,
Another boy.

I don't ever cry.
I am a hero, not a crybaby!
But why is it, Mother, why
Do the tears cry by themselves?

[*Note*: Nurit is a girl's name. In Hebrew, it is the name of a red flower, buttercup, of the genus *ranunculus*. This is significant for the interpretation of the poem. The above translation of the poem is literal, not literary; it does not contain the original patterns of rhyme and meter. A literary translation often deviates from the original diction and structure for reasons of alliteration, rhyme, syntax, etc. Thus, a literal translation was deemed more suitable here, as the original diction and structures are essential to the interpretation of the poem. Similarly, the translation of the Hebrew word *imma* as "Mother" rather than the more common "Mom" is for reasons that will be explained later.]

THE POEM'S SURFACE, EPIDERMIC LAYER

The narrator of the poem is the child Danny. This rhetorical strategy dictates the cognitive nature of the epidermic layer that is congruent with its official target reader, the child. Accordingly, Danny, the child narrator and protagonist, naïvely responds to his mother's model of behavior, which expects him to be a hero, to be clever, and not to cry "like a little fool." Naturally, Danny does not wish to be a "little fool." He does wish, though, to be a hero, to be clever, to conform to his mother's model of behavior, and to meet her expectations. In other words, Danny internalizes his mother's code of behavior while avoiding any cognitive dissonance with her.

Cognitive dissonance means a conflict between the mother's code and expectations and his own capability to obey and internalize that code and to meet those expectations. On the surface, Danny desperately wishes to avoid this kind of conflict. Nevertheless, Danny's painful experience with Nurit causes him to deviate from his mother's model. Thus, while Danny relates the chronicles of the painful incident, he unconsciously enlists a powerful technique of psychological rhetoric with which he tries to soften the impact of his failure.

Danny opens and concludes his "incriminating confession" with declarations that both deny his weakness and obey his mother's expectations. "I do not ever cry. /I am a hero, not a crybaby." The beginning and concluding points in any communication and discourse create an effective rhetorical-psychological impact. As Danny opens and concludes his "incriminating confession" with deliberate statements that display a declarative obedience to his mother's precepts, he manages (from the child-reader's point of view) to soften his deviation from his mother's model, to decrease its magnitude, and to emphasize his ability to meet her expectations. The message, which is delivered to the child, the official reader of the poem, is thus loud and clear; Danny is clever; he is a hero and not a crybaby despite the tears in his eyes. Thus, Danny's tears are relatively insignificant and are nothing but a temporary display of a short-lived weakness that does not undermine Danny's ability to live up to his mother's expectations. Certainly, from the child's standpoint, the separation between the tears and Danny, and the denial of a causal connection between the two, reinforces the message of the surface layer of the poem: that Danny is indeed a hero and a clever boy, that Danny does live up to his mother's model, despite his short-lived tearful reaction to the encounter with Nurit.

The division of roles is also clear and evident; Nurit is "the bad guy" while Danny's mother is "the good guy." Nurit is the obstacle to Danny's compliance with his mother's code and a hindrance to meeting her expectations. The mother is certainly "the good guy" on the surface layer of the poem; her behavior seems right and worthy, and her expectations are appropriate and fitting. However, the latent layer of the poem, the one addressing the adult, provides an encounter with a very different Danny and a very different mother.

THE POEM'S LATENT LAYER

What changes on the poem's latent layer? The narrator is still Danny and the mother still maintains her behavioral model, as well as her demanding expectations. However, Danny's reaction to his mother's model and expectations changes dramatically. The poem's surface layer aims to provide a congruency between Danny's behavior and personality and his mother's behavioral model and expectations. Following this vein, the surface layer suggests that Danny's tears are of insignificant, ephemeral nature and, thus, cast no shadow on his ability to meet his mother's demanding expectations. Thus, the surface layer denies any cognitive dissonance between Danny and his mother.

Despite the tears, Danny fully internalizes his mother's code, and neither he nor his mother has a reason to be upset or disappointed. The import of the latent layer, however, is dramatically different.

In the latent layer of the poem, one may discern a daring attempt by Danny to pursue a process of individuation. Through this process, Danny separates himself from his mother's code of behavior while realizing that the nature of his personality calls for a different code. Danny, therefore, is introduced to a cognitive dissonance between himself and his mother, since there is a gap between the mother's behavioral model and expectations and his own capacity to act accordingly.

While tracing Danny's psychological and emotional process, the adult reader encounters a Danny and a mother who are evidently different from the Danny and the mother of the poem's surface layer. She is not "the good mother," a source of worthy, commendable self-discipline, but rather "the bad mother," a parental figure who is not sufficiently sensitive to her son's vulnerable personality, an almost oppressive mother who forces on her son a tough model that does not suit him. He cannot fulfill her demanding expectations.

Danny of the latent layer also differs from Danny of the surface layer. On the one hand, he still tries to appease his mother and to please her, as he does in the surface layer. He still tries to overcome the cognitive dissonances that banish him from the safe domain of his mother's approval and appreciation. After all, his self-esteem greatly depends on his mother's acceptance and appreciation.

On the other hand, this Danny realizes that his personality does not fit his mother's model of behavior, and her demanding expectations are beyond his capability. The cognitive dissonance is too obvious to ignore. Thus, Danny is trapped by the conflict between his mother's expectations and his own faculties. He tries to extricate himself from his mother's oppressive model of behavior and to free himself from her demands.

Danny does not complete the process of individuation; such a process may be completed by a young adult only in years to come. Also, Danny's "long journey," exposing the real Danny, is not completed either. Danny's self-awareness is probably more intuitively than verbally formulated. Nonetheless, on a psychological-emotional level, Danny of the latent layer is much more daring and honest than Danny of the surface layer. He dares to admit that he is different from the person his mother wants him to be.

The opening stanza, which states the mother's code and her challenging expectations, may be read, on the surface, as a code of behavior established by a parent for a child. However, the following stanza reveals that this is not only a general code but also a specific reaction to Danny's crying. The transition, from a general code of behavior to a response to a specific incident, underlines the code's rigid demanding nature.

It is quite clear that the mother is using her behavioral model primarily to restrain the crying and to teach the child a moral lesson rather than to comfort him. The fact that the mother suggests that Danny might possibly be "a little fool" confirms and underlines the strict nature of her reaction. The mother does not offer compassion or comfort, but instead offers a demanding model of behavior. Any deviation from it results in Danny being "a little fool."

In light of this, it is no wonder that the mother refers to Danny in the third person ("my child") instead of the second person ("you"). The third-person rhetoric, which is the most formal and impersonal, well suits the strict, stern response of the mother to her son's crying. Thus, the poem's implied author (following Wayne C. Booth's terminology) uses effective rhetorical devices to emphasize the harsh nature of the mother's model, as well as her demanding expectations.

As already mentioned, Danny's reaction to his mother's demanding code and expectations—in the latent level of the poem—reveals a rejection at the same time that he is going through a process of individuation and increasing self-awareness. Again, Danny is probably not aware of this process on a verbal-cognitive level. His awareness is probably of an intuitive nature and in a formative stage.

Nevertheless, in the latent level of the poem, Danny's sense of discomfort with regard to his mother's stern demands is translated into a cognitive dissonance that reflects his increasing awareness of the gap between his personal abilities and his mother's code and expectations. Through this psychological-emotional process, Danny becomes self-aware and separates from his mother while cultivating an independent self-concept. This cognitive process of individuation and increasing self-awareness has three stages.

In the first stage, Danny of the latent layer does not differ from Danny of the surface layer. He denies his crying altogether: "I do not ever cry." Only toward the end of the stanza does the adult reader discover that Danny's denial is not only of a general nature, but it relates to a specific incident, his upsetting encounter with Nurit. At this first stage, however, Danny's denial—which is indeed a deliberate deviation from truth—expresses his strong desire to meet his mother's expectations. The cognitive dissonance between him and his mother is still too hard to admit, and the individuation process still calls for a breakthrough.

The second stage of the process marks the first crack in Danny's earlier denial: "I am not a crybaby," he maintains. On the one hand, Danny does not yet admit to the tears that resulted from his frustrating encounter with Nurit. On the other hand, he seems to withdraw from his previous rhetoric. By arguing that he is not a crybaby, Danny no longer denies that he has cried. He insists that he does not cry easily, but the notion of crying is no longer denied. Thus, Danny's statement, "I am not a crybaby" can be understood in the following fashion: although Danny argues that he does not cry easily, he no longer denies that crying is sometimes justified.

Of course, Danny is unable to verbalize this feeling, yet it is safe to interpret Danny's statement in this way. Danny shows more self-awareness. He no longer pretends that he does not "ever cry," though he does not yet admit that he cried because of Nurit. Even this slim crack in Danny's previous reaction to his mother's precepts indicates progress in Danny's process of individuation. In contrast to his mother's behavioral model, Danny seems to argue that there are circumstances that allow crying without risk of being labeled "a little fool."

Danny's earlier acceptance of his mother's strict code is less evident now. He realizes that crying is not absolutely negative. He recognizes the fact that his own personality and emotional make-up may not be in full agreement with his mother's moral code. Here, the cognitive dissonance between Danny and his mother comes to the fore for the first time, however hesitantly. This process can be viewed as one of gradual discovery of integrity. After his first denial of crying, Danny's integrity does not allow him to adhere for too long to a false story. He gradually retracts his previous denial and moves toward the truth. The truth is not only of a concrete nature, regarding Danny's tears, but it is also of a psychological-emotional nature: he objects to his mother's code of behavior and to her expectations.

In the third stage of the process, Danny transforms his initial deceitful denial (first stage) into a truthful confession: "It is just the tears...the tears... they / Cry by themselves." Danny, who previously denied ever crying, is currently confessing to having shed real tears. He makes progress when he shifts from the second stage to the third; not only does he admit having a legitimate reason for crying (second stage), he admits to actually crying, something he earlier denied.

Indeed, Danny attempts to transfer the blame from himself to his tears. In other words, Danny admits to crying while trying to free himself from the responsibility for crying. He is still a child who wishes to appease his mother. After all, a full process of individuation, as well as a full recognition of a cognitive dissonance and its implications, are certainly beyond the capabilities of a young child. Thus, whatever Danny realizes is mostly on an intuitive-emotional level rather than on a rationally, verbally formulated level. Nonetheless, Danny proves his integrity. As if his integrity cannot bear even a slight deviation from the truth, he decides to take responsibility for his tears. That responsibility is taken indirectly by

Danny through his narration of the events that resulted in his crying.

A close reading of the following two stanzas (stanzas three and four), which contain Danny's report of his painful encounter with Nurit, will help us understand his reaction to his mother's code. First, what is the deep meaning of that encounter, and what poetic means (selection of themes, composition and rhetoric) are used to express that meaning?

Second, what "doomed" Danny to failure in his encounter with the girl and in his inability to meet his mother's demands? Answering the last question re-acquaints the adult reader with the difference between the poem's "two mothers": the good mother of the surface layer, who rightly challenges her son with a worthy model of behavior, and the bad mother of the latent layer, who is not sufficiently sensitive to her son's psychological-emotional state as she forces her strict behavioral model on him.

It is clear that Danny's attempt to approach Nurit has some sexual implications. One may debate, however, how compelling they are. Sexuality, after all, is not limited to adults only, and young children, too, express a sense of sexuality. The fact that in the encounter, the male, Danny, approaches the female, Nurit, with an apple—the Biblical symbol of sexual temptation—and also with a flower—a traditional symbol of erotic courting—manifests and reinforces the erotic nature of the encounter. Furthermore, Nurit "betrays" Danny, going to play with another boy—which is twice repeated in this stanza. The verb "to play" (lesahek) contains sexual connotations (in Biblical Hebrew, it actually has sexual designation). (9) In view of all this, the adult reader may interpret Danny's disappointing experience with Nurit as a sexual as well as a social one.

The double nature of Danny's failure is reflected in another way. He fails to meet Nurit's demands, just as he fails to meet his mother's expectations. In fact, it is Danny's own nature that proves an obstacle to earning Nurit's affection and his mother's appreciation. The following consideration of stanzas three and four, in which Danny reports his failure, both rationalizes and reinforces the fact that Danny is doomed to fail: the gap between his nature and the nature of Nurit and his mother does not permit any other outcome. As noted earlier, the flower and the apple have clear erotic implications. The apple, in particular, is associated with male-female congress due to the Biblical allusion.

Danny's erotic failure has two components: composition and selection. As for composition, Danny gives Nurit the apple only after giving her the flower. Consequently, the act of giving an apple, the more erotic gesture, is delayed, coming after the somewhat less erotic, more romantic gesture of offering a flower. Thus, Danny displays a preference for the less erotic symbol. That preference is poetically manifested by composition, i.e., by the order of the presentation. From an erotic standpoint, Danny's preference to postpone and suspend the giving of the apple does not enhance his appeal. As for selection, Danny again fails to earn an erotic appeal. While he describes in detail the flower, which is the weaker erotic symbol, he offers no description of the apple, the stronger erotic symbol. The flower receives three descriptive adjectives: small, pretty, and blue, while the apple receives none. In fact, he "robs" the apple of its traditional color red (red being a salient symbol of eroticism).

Furthermore, by bestowing on the flower the color blue, Danny reduces its erotic potency. The color blue, as J.E. Cirlot points out, traditionally stands for "rational atmosphere," for "thinking," "devotion," and "innocence." Cirlot further maintains that the blue flower is a "legendary symbol of the impossible."

Thus, all symbolic connotations associated with the color blue—notably, blue flowers—stand in contrast to sensual passion and sexual lust. By endowing the flower with the color blue, Danny further weakens its initial romantic import. To sum up, then, Danny's erotic failure regarding his giving Nurit first a flower and then an apple has multiple significance. He gives the flower before he gives the apple. He does not describe the apple while giving the flower three adjectives. He robs the apple of its most traditional attribute, the red color, which in itself suggests eroticism. He endows the flower with a color that negates erotic associations. In other words, Danny "dilutes" the sexual aspects of both the apple and the flower. In both composition and selection, he makes errors that diminish the erotic import.

At this point in the reading process, the adult reader cannot overlook the widening gap between Danny and Nurit. It is not a coincidence that he uses the same adjective to describe the flower, *katon* (little) that his mother used earlier: "My child will never cry/ Like a little fool" (*petty katon*). This is a subtle verbal reference to the conflict between his personality and his mother's code of behavior.

The name Nurit in Hebrew denotes a red flower—*ranunculus* in Latin; it derives from the Aramaic noun *nur* (fire). However, Danny's blue flower—like his apple, which is not red—does not suit the "red" Nurit. They both lack erotic drive that is demanded by Nurit, as both her name and reaction prove. Thus, Danny's rejection by Nurit, although upsetting, is to be expected. But the way in which Nurit rejects Danny's clumsy approach is conveyed by intriguing rhetoric: "Nurit ate the apple/ She threw the flower in the yard..."

The rhetorical device used here can be described as "compositional chiasmus" (derived from the Greek letter X [*chi*], i.e., inversion or reversal of the order of presentation. [Cf. Samuel Johnson's verse: "For we that live to please, must please to live."] As for Danny, first he gives Nurit the flower and only later the apple. Nurit's reaction, however, upsets this order. She eats the apple first and only later does she throw the flower away. This compositional chiasmus is illustrated by the following formula:

Danny		Nurit
Act No. 1	"I gave Nurit a flower"	"Nurit ate the apple"
x		
Act No. 2	"I gave Nurit an apple"	"Nurit threw the flower"

One could safely argue that this pattern of compositional chiasmus has rhetorical merit, since any deviation from a previously established pattern yields a sense of rhetorical flexibility. However, that compositional chiasmus also has aesthetic merit. Due to the compositional chiasmus, the reader first learns that Nurit "ate the apple." Only later does the reader learn that Nurit also "threw the flower."

The act of eating the apple may be interpreted in a symbolic way. As the apple is the traditional symbol of erotic attraction and temptation (based on the Biblical allusion), the fact that the courted female eats the apple implies sexual willingness. The fact that an act of eating has sexual connotation (in Jewish tradition, many years before Freud: see, for instance, the Talmudic tractate Nedarim 20 b, 21: "I set for him a table and he turned it over," i.e., I was willing to have sexual intercourse) reinforces the notion that by eating the proffered apple, the female declares her erotic compliance.

As the adult reader learns that "Nurit ate the apple," he/she may make some assumptions regarding Nurit's attitude toward Danny; the reader is encouraged to presume that the act of eating the apple offered by Danny indicates a future acceptance of Danny's courtship. The surprise, then, comes when this expectation is frustrated. As soon as Nurit eats the apple, she throws away the flower and goes to play with another boy (the romantic betrayal is underscored by the erotic connotation of the Hebrew verb "to play"). The optimistic expectations are thus frustrated and denied.

The reader is misled rhetorically. The aesthetic merit of this rhetorical device is evident. The surprise resulting from the frustrated expectations focuses on Nurit's rejection of Danny and, thus, points the reader's attention to Danny's disappointment and distress, as well as to the gaps existing between him and Nurit, and between him and his mother's code. In the context of this disappointment, the mother's code and her expectations seem almost oppressive.

Danny confession comes to an end. The conclusion of Danny's confession reaches a climactic point in his long journey into self-awareness. His process of individuation is hesitant but consistent. His initial stubborn denial turns into a candid recognition. He does not deny his tears anymore; in touching rhetoric, he narrates the origin of the tears. Through the process of individuation, Danny exposes what his mother aims to erase; his mother's *modus operandi* is not even a *modus vivendi* on his part.

Danny is just a little child. He is not old enough to carry for long the burden of a cognitive dissonance with his mother. Her role in his self-esteem is too prominent to be denied. He cannot afford to lose her affection. A complete self-awareness is too consuming at Danny's age and should be delayed for much later. A sustained conflict with parental expectation is untenable at Danny's stage of emotional development. Thus, Danny's natural drive to appease his mother trumps his recently found integrity. He withdraws from a position of opposition to his mother's code and calls for her disapproval. As if intimidated by the realization that he does not measure up to her expectations, he "escapes" to his previous safe place, to his initial "rhetorical ammunition," the total denial: "I do not ever cry / I am a hero, not a crybaby."

It is interesting that Danny calls himself "a hero," the same epithet that his mother used earlier: "My child is a hero..." This fact underlines Danny's desire to re-earn his mother's approval by following her model of behavior while extricating himself from the conflict in which he is trapped.

However, the Danny who ends the poem arguing, "I do not ever cry," is not the same Danny who opened the poem with the statement, "I do not ever cry." Despite his return to the initial denial, he cannot fully escape the sobering experience of his individuation process through which he has acquired some self-awareness. Danny may keep denying, but he cannot free himself of his self-awareness nor erase it. Thus, he realizes again that a total deceitful denial is not workable any more. Danny is truly trapped.

On the one hand, a total denial of crying seems a convenient vehicle to re-earn his mother's approval. On the other hand, his recently gained self-awareness does not allow a total denial. Danny is caught between the hammer and the anvil, between the way he is and the way his mother wants him to be. No compromise, no common denominator is available. In his distress, he addresses his mother directly for the first time. "But why is it, Mother, why / Do the tears cry by themselves?"

One can hear in Danny's voice a plea, a frustration, even an accusation. The burden of a cognitive dissonance is too much for him. The fact that a reference to the mother both opens and concludes the poem is deliberate. It creates a sense of circularity that evokes Danny's dead-end situation. He is encircled, imprisoned by his mother's ethics and by his own standards, which are in conflict.

There are two Dannys in the poem: Danny of the surface layer, who willingly internalizes his mother's code and meets her expectations despite the incident with Nurit, and Danny of the latent layer, who wrestles with the conflict between his psychological faculties and his mother's code. The latent Danny faces a cognitive dissonance through a painful process of individuation. Danny of the surface layer is aimed at the official reader of the poem, the child, whereas Danny of the latent layer is aimed at the unofficial reader, the adult. While the boy in the poem becomes two, the two females in the poem, Nurit and the mother, become one: they both emasculate Danny and they are both impervious to his sensitivity and distress.

In the last decades, feminists have fought to eliminate gender discrimination. However, men, too, have suffered deprivation and have been robbed of the right to be sensitive and vulnerable. In this respect, Nurit seems to behave in the tradition of *la belle dame sans merci*, weakening and emasculating Danny. She does it through eroticism, while the mother does so by forcing on him traditional masculine roles and macho expectations. Between these two females, Danny is left powerless, besieged by the mother's code and by Nurit's rejection. Yet, Danny is not alone; he is joined by one more Danny, a third one, who is allusive and Biblical, harkening back three thousand years. This third character invades the poem and joins his younger poetic peer.

THE POEM'S CRYPTIC-ALLUSIVE LAYER: BIBLICAL ALLUSION

> *I never understood Samson's hair;*
> *That might hidden in it; its ascetic secrecy*
> *The prohibition (that should not be condemned)*
> *to discuss it;*

The constant fear of losing the braids, the
endless fear
When Delilah caresses them softly…
  —Nathan Zach, "Samson's Hair"

As mentioned earlier, the poem's cryptic layer metaphorically reflects its latent layer. These two layers form the poem's deep structure that secludes the child, the official reader, while addressing the unofficial reader, the adult. Addressing the adult reader on multiple levels through two rhetorical vehicles which echo each other, leads to the unique deeper structure and important meaning of the poem. The importance of the deep structure does not emerge despite the conflict between it and the upper structure but rather because of that conflict. The poem's implied author invites the adult reader to bypass the simplified upper level and focus on the intricate aesthetics of the deep structure as well as on its educational message. Thus, the implied author introduces an extra allusive layer not only in order to enrich the aesthetics of the deep structure but also to better express its urgent moral.

The implied author's desire that the adult reader will appreciate the cryptic-allusive layer is manifest in the poem's title, "Danny the Hero" (*Danny Gibor*). The traditional designation of the Biblical Samson is "Samson the Hero" (*Shimshon Hagibor*). Even children will easily identify the allusion to the Biblical Samson.

However, the allusion in the title is only the tip of the allusive iceberg. There are several other references that connect Danny to Samson. While the majority of allusions are obvious, some are less conspicuous, but they are no less meaningful as they help corroborate and reinforce the allusive system.

Moreover, the common denominators shared by Danny and Samson go beyond a cluster of local allusions. The allusive analogy between Danny and Samson also has more general ramifications. Samson, like Danny, is a victim of behavioral code and challenging expectations, which he fails to meet. Both Danny and Samson lack the capability to satisfy the demands imposed on them. In this respect, one could refer to the allusive system that connects Danny to Samson as "rhetorical bait" or a signpost that draws the adult reader's attention to the essence of the affinity between Danny and Samson. Their attempt to live up to the behavioral norms imposed upon them is doomed to failure.

The allusion to Samson in the title *Danny Gibor* becomes firmer in view of the fact that the name *Dan*—from which Danny derives—is associated with Samson. Samson belongs to the tribe of Dan. The *Book of Judges* presents Samson as a Danite, belonging to the Dan family (*Mishpahat Hadany*; Judges 13.2). Thus, Samson's two epithets, the hero and the Danite, are both represented in the title of the poem.

The name of Nurit also carries an allusion to Samson. Nurit is a red flower whose name derives from *Nur*, meaning fire. The name Samson (*Shimshon* in Hebrew) is also associated with fire, as the etymology of the name connects it to the Hebrew noun Shemesh, meaning sun.

Moreover, many chronicles of Samson involve references to fire. Before Samson's birth, his parents sacrificed a burnt offering to God. In this context, the word "flame" (*lahav*) is mentioned twice (Judges, 13.20). The Philistines threaten to burn Samson's first wife and set her father's house on fire (ibid, 14.15). Samson's furious retaliation is done with fire; he ties burning torches to the tails of three hundred foxes and sets them free, causing a huge fire that burns the Philistines' fields (ibid. 15.6)

Another time, Samson exhibits his unusual strength by tearing the ropes with which his own people had bound him. The narrator uses a fire simile: "...and the ropes on his arms became like flax that catches fire; the ropes melted off his hands." When Samson frees himself from the ropes with which Delilah has bound him, the fire metaphor is repeated: "he pulled the tendons apart, as a strand of tow comes apart at the touch of fire. (ibid. 16.9).

Another link between the poem and Samson's story has to do with parental figures. As we wrote earlier, Danny's mother is mentioned only at the beginning and at the end of the poem, two strategic rhetorical points that call for much attention. The same applies to Samson's parents; the parents open the story and the father (and his brothers) concludes it. Thus, in both cases, the parental figure encircles the story. Both Danny and Samson are surrounded by parental expectations that they fail to meet.

Another interesting allusion binding the two texts together has to do with alliteration. The Philistines ask both Samson's wife and Delilah to prevail upon him to disclose the answer to his riddle and then to coax him to reveal the secret of his power (ibid 14.16; 16. 5.) In both cases, the word used is *patti* (imperative of the verb *lephatot*, singular, feminine, second person). The word *patti* is twice repeated in the Samson chronicle and thus merits our attention.

The use of *patti* in the Samson story suggests an alliterative affinity with *petty* (fool) used in the poem. Danny's mother says "My child will never cry /Like a little fool (petty)." The alliterative allusion that binds the two words becomes more evident in view of the fact that Samson, Danny's Biblical "twin," commits foolish acts while acting as a *petty*; his sexual attraction to loose women casts a shadow on his judgment and eventually leads to his demise. Perhaps this alliterative allusion, despite its poetic appeal, is not sufficiently solid by itself, but it joins other, more conclusive allusions.

Another interesting allusion hinges on childish characteristics shared by both Danny and Samson. When Samson is with Delilah, they play mother-child roles. Delilah pampers Samson as if he were a child. "She lulled him to sleep on her lap" (ibid 16.19). Similarly, the use of the word "to play" (*lesahek*) is used in both texts. Just as Nurit puts down Danny and then goes to play with another boy, the Philistines put down their prisoner Samson by ordering him to "play" in front of them (ibid. 16.5). In both texts, erotic connotations are associated with the verb *lesahek*, to play. Also, in both texts, the verb to play is related to female betrayal. Nurit betrays Danny and Delilah betrays Samson.

The number three seems to figure significantly in both texts as an allusive analogy. There are several sets of three in the Samson story. Samson sets fire to the Philistines' fields by setting free three hundred foxes carrying burning torches. Samson gathers thirty young men for his wedding party (ibid. 14.11) and he promises them thirty linen tunics and thirty sets of clothing "if they crack and decipher his riddle" (ibid.14.12). If they fail, they must give him "thirty linen tunics and thirty sets of clothing" (ibid. 14.13).

Later, "the spirit of the Lord gripped" Samson. "He went down to Ashkelon and killed thirty of its men" (ibid. 14. 15). The Philistines blame the people of Judah for Samson's "guerilla" attacks, whereupon "three thousand men of Judea" imprison Samson and threaten "to hand him over to the Philistines." (ibid.15.11). When Samson is forced by the Philistines "to play" in front of them, "three thousand men and women on the roof" watch him. (ibid, 16.15).

The number three seems to dominate Samson's married life, too. Samson had three women: his first wife the Philistine, the harlot of Gaza, and Delilah. Moreover, Delilah levels this accusation at Samson. "This makes three times that you have deceived me and have not told me what makes you so strong" (ibid. 16.15).

The presence of the number three in the poem is no less significant. Danny, we have seen, goes through a process of individuation in which he discovers that his psychological and emotional faculties are in conflict with his mother's code, which in turn reaches an independent self-awareness that leads to a cognitive dissonance. His process of individuation evolves in three stages: total denial of crying ("I do not ever cry"); a partial denial of crying while admitting to a certain legitimacy for crying ("I am not a crybaby"); and a full recognition of crying while attempting to transfer the responsibility to the tears themselves ("It is just the tears... the tears.../ they cry by themselves...")

Danny's encounter with Nurit has three stages as well: giving Nurit a flower; giving Nurit an apple; giving Nurit "everything." Similarly, Nurit's response has three stages: eating the apple; discarding the flower; going to play with another boy. However, the allusive analogy between Danny's story and Samson's chronicles is even more detailed and intricate.

Danny's three encounters with Nurit echo Samson's three encounters with women. In the first encounter with Nurit, Danny gives her a blue flower. The color blue, as noted earlier, stands for rational thinking and intellectual faculties. The same can be said of Samson's encounter with his first wife, who requests that he provide her with the reasoning behind his riddle. This reasoning stands for thinking and intellectual faculties. The Biblical narrator implies that Samson chose a Philistine wife, not for love but, rather, as a ploy to gain information about the Philistines' plot against Israel (ibid. 14.4). Thus, Danny's first encounter with Nurit parallels Samson's interaction with his first wife. In both cases there is an intellectual component.

In the second encounter with Nurit, Danny gives her an apple, the traditional symbol of sexual attraction. An erotic attraction is also the ground for Samson's interaction with his second woman, the prostitute.

In the third encounter with Nurit, Danny says: "I gave (her) everything." This is exactly what Samson does in his encounter with the third woman, Delilah; he tells her the secret of his power, which is, indeed, everything for him.

By revealing the secret of his power to her, Samson gives her himself, his existence, his life.

Thus, Danny's three encounters with Nurit reflect, metaphorically, Samson's three encounters with his women—the parallels are very noticeable. Danny fails. So does Samson. They both succumb under romantic circumstances. Danny stumbles because of his hesitation and weakness, and Samson stumbles because he fails to curb his erotic disposition. They both fail to stand up to demanding emasculating women. For both Danny and Samson, *cherchez la femme* proves to be the cause of their downfall. Danny faces a parental behavior model and demanding expectations that conflict with his personality and with his emotional temperament. And the same applies to Samson. Even before his birth, he was expected to be a Nazarite, consecrated to God: no razor could touch his hair, and he was destined to deliver Israel from the oppression of the Philistines (ibid. 13.5)

However, Samson's personality did not accord with his high calling. His attraction to foreign women (Delilah is no better than the harlot, as the etymology of her name indicates: a devious woman) was a breach of his Nazarite status. His hair, which should not be touched by a razor, is shamefully shaved by Delilah. Nor did he fulfill the national aspirations; despite some local victories over the Philistines, he failed to deliver his people from the Philistine oppression. In fact, Samson's raids against the Philistines worsened the situation so much that the people of Judah planned to extradite Samson to the Philistines (ibid. 15.12). Many of Samson's heroic acts did little to alleviate the national distress.

Here is a verse from a poem by David Avidan, a contemporary Israeli poet, which despite its cynical, ironic tone is relevant to our discussion. "Samson was probably not the wisest of men." The childish nature of some of his exploits—reinforced by the image of him sleeping like a child in Delilah's lap—underscores the analogy between him and Danny. By the same token, Danny, the protagonist of the poem's latent layer, seems like a childlike incarnation of his Biblical counterpart, the protagonist of the poem's cryptic, allusive layer. The poem has only one narrator, and yet that single narrator consists of a triple rhetorical stratification. One Danny addresses the poem's official reader (the child) while the other two, Danny of the latent layer and Samson the Danite of the poem's cryptic-allusive layer, address the unofficial reader, the adult reader. The message conveyed by the two Dannys of the poem's deep structure is the focus of the adult reader's attention.

One may debate over the educational implications suggested by the poem's contradictory message. Why is the official reader, the child, introduced to an educational message that is not only at odds with the poem's latent educational message but also one that is not appreciated by the poem's implied author? Do the child's cognitive limitations—that prevent him from a full realization of the text and its deep structure—legitimize his being approached with an educational credo that calls for resentment and criticism? Is the adult reader - who reads the poem to the child or guides the child's reading of the poem -expected by the implied author to acquaint the child with the latent, desirable educational message of the poem?

Certainly, from a psychological-educational standpoint, these questions call for further analysis. However, from a poetic point of view, the oxymoronic rhetorical tendencies of the poem produce an intriguing tension: the poem's unique aesthetic quality is derived from its split, multi-layered, contradictory character. Thus, we have here three Dannys, two mothers, and one evident poetic merit.

The chronicles of Danny the Hero and his allusive peer, Samson the Danite the Hero, may be considered—albeit with some reservations—as another version of the Aquedah story (the Biblical story of the sacrifice of Isaac. Aquedah in Hebrew means binding). The altar in this case is a parental behavioral model. The parents' expectations are too demanding for the children, denying their needs, ignoring their personality structures, and overlooking their abilities. Daughters and sons of different age groups are almost compelled to bind themselves to that altar, and they are doomed to failure.

A much-respected figure in contemporary Israeli poetry, Yehuda Amichai, begins one of his better known poems with the following verse: "The real hero of the aquedah was the ram" (that was sacrificed instead of Isaac). The real heroes of the two aquedah chronicles, Danny and Samson, are neither Danny of the poem's surface layer nor Samson of the prevailing tradition; the real heroes of these two aquedah chronicles are Danny the "disobedient" child, and his allusive-Biblical counterpart, the childish Samson: two anti-heroes who are bound to the same exacting, behavioral altar. "The angel went home," says Amichai's poem, and "...Abraham and God left a long time ago." But Danny and Samson stay bound to altars of challenging expectations that they can never meet, hounded by a code of behavior that is alien to their psychological profile, banished from their natural element.

NOTES

1. Cf. Constantine Ceorgiou, *Children and Their Literature*, New Jersey:Prentice-Hall, 1969) p. 51.

2. Cf. Zohar Shavit, *Poetics of Children's Literature*, Athens and London: Georgia University Press, 1986.

3. Cf. James Steel Smith, *A Critical Approach to Children's Literature* (New York: McGraw-Hill, 1967), p.15.

4. Cf. Paul Heins, "Coming to Terms With Criticism", in *Children and Literature: Views and Review*, edited by Virginia Haviland (Brighton: Scott, Forseman, 1973), p. 408.

5. Cf. Bruno Bettleheim, *The Uses of Enchantment* (New York 1976).

6. Ibid. 41.

7. Ibid. 42.

8. Cf. Miriam Yalan-Stekelis, "Yesh Lee Sod" (*I have a Secret*, in Hebrew) (Tel Aviv, 41). A brief discussion of this poem is included in a book by Miri Baruch and Maya Fruchtman, *Every Poem Has a Name* (in Hebrew) (Tel Aviv: Papyrus, Tel Aviv University, 1982), pp. 56-58. I discuss this poem, in Hebrew, in my study: Yair Mazor: *"Danny the Hero or Samson of Dan?"* Ma'gley Keri'a 22 (1993) pp. 9-20.

9. See, for instance, Genesis 20.9: "And Sarah saw the son of Hagar the Egyptian , whom she had conceived with Abraham, playing..." Ismael displays sexual maturity and therefore threatens Isaac's primacy. This is why Sarah demands that Abraham send away both Hagar and Ismael. See also the false allegations of rape that Potiphar's wife brings against Joseph "A Hebrew man was brought to play with us and he came to lie with me and I cried with a loud voice." (Genesis 39.14).

10. A literary allusion is a pattern consisting of at least two components: the allusive component in the text at hand and the alluded component anchored in another text (usually of a literary nature). Once the reader encounters the allusive component, he/she cannot overlook the analogy between the allusive component and its counterpart embedded in another text (which is presumably recognizable by an educated reader). Thus, the pattern of literary allusion is founded on three components: the signifier (the allusive

component), the signified (the alluded component) and the analo-
gous-allusive interaction between the two (activated by the reader's
realization). The potential aesthetic function of the literary allusion
has a double nature. The first one: the signified element, while
triggered by the signifying element, endows the text with its own
connotations and therefore enriches the allusive text. The second is
of reverse character. Due to differences between the signifying
element and the signified element, a touch of irony emerges and
bestows on the allusive text a sense of ambiguity and complexity.
The nature of literary allusions is discussed in the following
studies:

Ziva Ben-Porat, "The Poetics of Literary Allusions," PTL (1979: p.
108; "Reader, Text and Literary Allusions: On realizations of
Literary Allusions." (in Hebrew) Hasifrut 26 (1978) pp. 1-25).

Yair Mazor, "Selective Utilizations of Allusive Materials in Poetry" (in
Hebrew) Rosh, 2 (1978 pp.23-27; "Making Poetry and Politics: Dalia
Rabikovitz's "One Cannot Kill a Baby Twice" (in Hebrew), Iton 77, 8
no. 83 (1986) pp. 18-19, 36. The last two articles are included in
the book by Yair Mazor: A Sense of Structure. See also, Mazor, Not
by Poem Alone: David Fovel's Art of Narrative, pp. 63-68.

11. Yaakova Sacerdoti: *Together and Separately as Well: On Adult and
Child Addressees in the Discourse of Children's Literature,*
Hakibbutz Hameuchad, Tel Aviv, 2000.

SAUL TCHERNICHOVSKY: INTRODUCTORY COMMENT

Next to the poet Haim Nachman Bialik (1873-1934), Saul Tchernichovsky (1875-1943) was the great poet of Hebrew letters at the end of the Revival Movement and the beginning of the modern period. Apart from being a prolific poet, Tchernichovsky was also an accomplished translator, who translated world masterpieces into Hebrew from English, French, German, ancient Greek, and Acadian ("The Epic of Gilgamesh" and "The Creation of the World" from the Babylonian Epic "Kalawalla").

A physician by profession, Tchernichovsky also wrote books and articles on medicine. He was born in Russia and, after completing his medical studies in Heidelberg and Lausanne (in 1907), he went back to Russia. In the First World War, he served as a military doctor. In 1919-1922 he lived in Odessa, then moved to Germany and, in 1931, immigrated to Palestine. His first poems are marked by naiveté, pathos, and spontaneous identification with the cosmos. Many of his poems were influenced by Nietzsche's philosophy and reflect his admiration for ancient Greek culture. He wrote lugubrious, expressive ballads and long idylls focusing on man's oneness with nature that nevertheless have tragic elements at their core.

SNOW WHITE DOES NOT LIVE THERE ANYMORE: SAUL TCHERNICHOVSKY'S CHILDREN'S STORIES

> *The childhood shows the man,*
> *As morning shows the day.*
> —Milton, *Paradise Regains*, Book IV, line 220

> *The child is father of the man.*
> —Wordsworth, "My Heart Leaps", Line 7

Saul Tchenichovsky's stories for children are clearly aimed at the formal addressee of the text, i.e., the child, but they do so without trying to win favors or sucking up to the child by ignoring the adult world or by circumventing the target audience of grown-ups, who are the informal addressees of the text.

In fact, it is quite the reverse. Tchernichovsky's stories make no attempt to create a barrier between the children's world and the adults' world. The message they impart to children is: everyone, children as well as adults, is part of the same world, responds to the same realities, and obeys the same rules and regulations, however fair or unfair they may be. There is no bias, no currying favors, no embellishment, only representation of reality as it is. This is true especially with regard to nature stories, which were collected in a separate volume entitled, *What Was and Was Not* (1942).

Even when the stories display conventions and behaviors traditionally associated with children's literature (which do not conform to the real world, such as talking animals or inanimate objects that exhibit independence and volition), the rules that govern them are still those of normative reality, where ugliness and suffering have their place.

A close reading of Tchernichovsky's children's stories reveals a poetic reality that is interesting not only by itself but one that reflects on the works he wrote for adults. Naturally, there are differences in the aesthetic conventions dictated by the different genres, but a "genetic" deep structure can be discerned underneath. This is true of any genuine artist. Take, for example, the paintings of Nachum Gutman; they reveal his genetic aesthetic hallmarks both in the illustration to his children's books and in his oil paintings whose target audience are adults. Similarly, there are distinct parallels between the various genres of Tchernichovsky's works for adults and for children.

The prose fiction Tchernichovsky wrote for adults is comprised of three genres, three modal patterns that derive from one prototype: Atmosphere fiction, Action fiction, and Love Fiction. In Atmosphere fiction, one usually finds extensive expositional retardation that spans over most of the story. The plot in this genre is deprived of its traditional prominent position and is relegated to the margins, to the periphery of the text. A "provocative poetics" interferes with the traditional balance between exposition and plot (which usually maintains that plot is dominant and exposition has an auxiliary, inferior function). Here the retardational exposition is of paramount importance because it contains the essence of the story.

The intention of Atmosphere fiction is to convey a certain social reality (which the plot reflects in more concrete terms), and to reflect the typical components of that reality.

Action fiction, on the other hand, focuses on the concrete and the unique. It usually eschews retardational expositions (that aims at the general and not the particular, which is preferred in Action fiction) and rejects the social criticism that typifies the Atmosphere fiction that inveighs against social ills. Action fiction tells a story.

Love fiction presents a third model, somewhere between the other two. Structurally, Love fiction is closer to Action fiction. For the most part it dispenses with exposition and focuses on the concrete and on the plot, which has a strong erotic component. However, some love stories do adopt an expository retardation, as is common in Atmosphere fiction. The latter, we noted, deals with social reality, criticizes it and aims at correcting its wrongs. Love fiction deals with universal, human, and psychological reality that concerns human erotic nature (except that here there is an acceptance, rather than denunciation of reality).

In Tchernichovsky's literature for adults, there are two distinct models, plus an additional model, a kind of mixture of the two. The deviation from the two standard models does not undermine them. The same is true about Tchernichovsky's children's stories.

There are no expository retardations in these children's stories. The reason for this is not the writer's rejection of his narrative inclination, but a deliberate and conscious avoidance. The target audience of children's literature does not call for retardational expositions. A child's attention span and power of abstraction are different from an adult's. The retardational exposition, that delays the main development and the plot is, thus, not suited for the concentration and focus of the young addressee. The tendency of the retardational exposition (in Tchernichovsky) to deal in abstract generalization does not accord with the predisposition of the young addressee to focus on the concrete and the immediate.

The absence of retardational exposition attests to the sensitivity of the author to the needs and abilities of the potential addressee. When you do find retardational exposition in a story for children, it is offset by a technique of cloaking the device: the external narrator invades the fictional world, announcing the upcoming arrival of the retardational exposition, explaining its introduction and pointing out the seam lines between it and the plot.

Thus, for example in "Timoshka:" "Because I want to tell you about Timoshka, I am obliged to deviate a little, as is my wont [in stories for adults—Y.M] and tell ..." We also find in Tchernichovsky's fiction for children—as well in his fiction for adults—the catalog structure, a presumed influence of the Greek epics, as well as a focus on the modest and humble, the powerless and marginal, the rejected and forgotten, and the underdog.

One category of children's literature is nature stories, stories that center around the animal and botanical kingdom. Animals are the protagonists of these stories; they talk, negotiate, argue, and act. Most of these stories are collected in a volume titled *What Was and Was Not*" (Yavneh, Tel Aviv1942). These nature stories resemble the Action stories for adults; here, too, the focus is on plot, action, and exploits. However, there is also noticeable similarity to Atmosphere fiction in the attempt to go beyond the concrete specific story of the plot to a broader generalization that aims at depicting and reforming social reality.

The nature stories deal with life on earth and its arbitrary laws, laws that are often unfair and unjust, where evil triumphs, where there is pain, suffering and deprivation. Examples are: the bereaved stork, destroyed by her own kind because her offspring are different ("Story about a Stork and Naughty Kids"); the stonefish evicted from their habitat ("The Stonefish"); the little stork punished by her mother for her original, unorthodox views ("Math Lesson"); unfair accusation aimed at a ball, not at those who threw it ("Everything in Proportion"; here, inanimate objects join the realm of flora and fauna); and the triumph of a parasitic spider, who feeds on other's misfortune and glories in its own stupidity ("The Spider").

In all these stories one finds critical generalizations and commentary on social reality and its laws. There is a lesson to be drawn, a moral, a message that make no attempt to gloss over the ugly unpleasant truth. Here and there in the stories one finds "spots of light" that alleviate the oppression of bitter reality: the collapse of the arrogant, spiteful airplane ("All in Good Measure"); or the death of the stuck up hubristic mouse ("In the Field"). But these exceptions only prove the rule: justice in this world is rare and hard to come by.

The nature stories contain a certain metaphoric, symbolic quality; the generalizations drawn from the animal world aim at the human world, they are representations, parables. Thus, young readers learn not only about the laws of nature, but the laws that govern their own lives. There is a link, then, between the children's nature stories and the Atmosphere stories for adults. Both of these genres present an outrageous, abominable reality. Snow White, at any rate, does not live there anymore. Perhaps she never lived there. (It is interesting to compare this tendency to the poems of Miriam Yalan-Stekelis, which also refuse to sugarcoat reality and emphasize its sadness and anguish.)

The second mode of Tchernichovsky's children's fiction is the Action stories. They are distinctly related to Action stories for adults. Here, too, the main focus is the plot, and autobiographical elements are an important part. Even if some autobiographical details are imagined, and not anchored in reality, they still bear the hallmark of autobiographical rhetoric. Such are the stories: "I catch tadpoles" (*Davar L'Yeladim*, No. 16, 8.1.42); "Once upon a Hannucka" (*Davar L'Yeladim*, No.12, 11.12.41); "No Matzo for Passover" (*Davar L'Yeladim*, No. 28-291.4.42); "Me With All The Challahs" (*Davar L'Yeladim*, No.37-38, 8.6.43); "Troubles Galore" (Davar L'Yeladim, No. 33, 6.5.43); "A Tale of a Pail and Itzi-Berke" (*Davar L'Yeladim* No. 27, 25.3.43); "The Beadle's Apples" (*Davar L'Yeladim*, No. 1-2, 13.10.43), and others.

The third narrative mode in Tchernichovsky's fiction for children is a combination of the two other modes (Nature stories and Action stories). In this intermediary category one finds the stories: "The Sparrow's Dance" (*Davar L'Yeladim*, No. 20, 4.2.43); "Canary" (*Davar L'Yeladim*, NO. 15, 31/12/42); "Golden Atonement" (*Davar L'Yeladim*, No. 10, 26.11.42), and others. The very titles of the stories suggest that they are nature stories. Indeed, all these stories were published under the title "My Animal Friends," and "My Winged Friends" (or "Fowl"). Each of these stories has an animal at the center of its plot. But here the affinity with nature stories ends and the trend toward Action stories begins.

While in the nature stories beasts and birds display anthropomorphism (personification), talk and act like humans, in the intermediate genre, the birds and the beasts are devoid of any human characterizations; they are described from the outside by an adult narrator who is reminiscing about his past. In the Nature stories, the creatures are shaped by the conventions of children's literature, which impart human qualities and capabilities to all the denizens inhabiting the realm of flora and fauna, including inanimate objects.

Not so in the intermediate mode: here one finds no fairy tale elements, and the beasts and the birds—despite their central position in the plot—follow the pattern of the real world. Similarly, one does not find general statements about objective reality in this category, and there is no attempt to exceed or transcend the limits of the plot or of the unique, specific story.

Thus, the tripartite division of literary modes that typifies Tchernichovsky's literature for adults (Atmosphere, Action, Love) is replicated in his other literary genre, children's literature. The same deep underlying structure that charts Tchernichovsky's adult literature, migrates to his children's literature and resides there.

A COUPLE OF EXAMPLES

The most aesthetically pleasing nature stories can be found in the collection "*What Was and Was Not*" (Yavne, Tel Aviv, 1942). These stories display maturity and insight in their artistic composition and in their conceptions and ideas. For instance, in the final story, "The Spider" (pp.34-39), the protagonist, the spider, possesses (within the fictional world of the text) human faculties and human consciousness: he thinks, hopes, expects, deliberates, doubts; he is happy when his fears dissipate and when his wishes are fulfilled.

In the collective conventional-traditional context, a spider is not a likable creature. In this story he is even less so. The spider in this story is exceedingly selfish, narcissistic, and repulsive. He is convinced that anything that happens around him is meant for his benefit and for his use. Throughout the story he has several encounters, which result in the downfall of others. He benefits from all of them and is reinforced in his belief that everything is done for his sake.

The poor gardener's labors improve the spider's meal; when the gardener is evicted by the king's servants and a palace is built on the confiscated land, the spider gets even better meals ("the spider stayed at home, amply provided with food. There were many servants around and the food was plentiful; so were the leftovers and the flies that swarmed and spawned." p .35.)

With every development of the plot, the haughty and egotistical spider gets more prosperous and powerful. He is convinced that everything that has taken place around him was done for him and for his benefit. The story ends tragically: the king's enemies kill the king and the queen, and destroy their palace where the spider has found refuge. The reader, who has been expecting the selfish spider's come-uppance, is impatient to read about his downfall; surely the destruction of the palace presages the demise of the spider, who is like the frog in Aesop's fable who puffed himself up in order to resemble an ox and ended up bursting and dying.

However, the reader's expectations are thwarted. The spider manages to survive the destruction of the palace and continues to thrive and to hold on to his selfish convictions.

> "Undisturbed, the spider spread his web along the remains of the wall, and sat there warming himself in the sun after dinner, thinking deep thoughts. In the end, whatever people do, they do for my benefit: they amass armies, shed blood, kill the king, destroy the palace, sack his treasures, leave no brick in place, and all this so that in my old age, I could enjoy the sun and finally breath fresh air!" (p. 39).

The legitimate expectations for the spider's downfall are frustrated and with them the simple naïve hope that evil will be punished, arrogance and hubris will be dispelled. The frog in Aesop's fable bursts to bits and the positive lesson is that he got his come-uppance, that his silly vanity was not rewarded. Not so in Tchernichovsky's tale.

As if to say: fairy tales are one thing, reality is another. Fables may be charming and captivating, but reality is something else.

The rhetorical structure of a plot, which encourages the reader to entertain certain expectations that will be thwarted later, in fact, exposes the intention of the implied narrator: not to lead the young reader astray; a reluctance to provide a deceptive, illusory reality; a determination to acquaint young readers with the disappointments and frustrations that life has in store for them. Other stories in *What Was and Was Not* have a similar message. The same is true of some of the stories in the composite genre ("Nellie" and "Golden Atonement"), which end on a note of "grown-up grief" (to use Leah Goldberg's apt phrase), a sober conclusion that introduces the youngster to the sorrows of this world.

Another example of a nature story is "A Story of a Stork and Naughty Children" (*What Was and Was Not*, pp. 5-8). Mischievous kids remove the stork's eggs from the nest and replace them with goose eggs. When the eggs hatch, the male stork is enraged, and beats the hatchlings to death with his bill. Then he turns to his mate and thrashes her furiously. "The farmer motioned to his son to go up on the roof and shoo away the angry bird. The son then picked up the bleeding wounded stork and took her home." (P.7) The stork recovers, spreads her wings and flies away. Then one day,

> "... there was a great commotion outside, shrieks
> and the din of clashing beaks like dry sticks...

*the storks were standing around the bereaved
stork raining blows on her with their beaks,
making a terrible ruckus. When the kids came
and dispersed the birds, they saw the stork lying
dead on the floor, her skull crushed."* (p 8)

In this story, as in "The Spider," a rhetorical pattern of thwarted expectation is present. When the stork survives the first time, one hopes for revival, rehabilitation, correction, since the reason for the attack on her, the foreign goslings that so enraged the male, have been removed. But this optimistic expectation is denied at the end of the story; the stork that escaped death at the beginning of the story ends up dead at the end. As far as her own kind are concerned, the stigma (of having a foreign brood) cannot be expunged or forgiven.

Again, we see here how Tchernichovsky chooses to focus on the rejected, the spurned, the outcast, the forgotten, and the different—those he chooses to bring to center stage. There are no fairy tale endings here; life has its own rules, which the author tries to convey.

There are other similarities and parallels between Tchernichovsky's stories for adults and his stories for children, as well as between the children's stories and his poetry. In the story "The Field" (*What Was and Was Not*, PP. 11-13), we encounter the motif of the stone slab, which is a recurrent image in Tchernichovsky's prairie poems.

In "The Field," a large statue stands on a desolate mound; "it was so ancient and so gloomy, like Time itself. And it looked beyond the field and the time. It seemed to be carved from the primordial rocks." (p 12) This is reminiscent of the poem "A Man is a Reflection."

> *"...In the vast expanse of the bluish prairie*
> *The sacred mounds dream on top of wondrous*
> *graves.*
> *No one knows who built them and when*
> *And who sleeps eternally in their bosom.*
> *Dusty idols for many generations...*
> *Overlooking gray, silent borders*
> *Like the prairie itself..."*
> [Compare also Bialik's "The Dead of the Desert".]

As, in other nature stories, "The Field" imparts a certain truth about life in general, which is underlined by the surprising ending. The hubris and presumption of the field mouse are suddenly cut short. "Before the little mouse could turn his head, the vulture sank his claws in him..." (p 13). Here, too, the narrator eschews any attempt to conceal or disguise the tragic aspects of existence and the laws that govern reality. Pride goes before a fall.

It is interesting to compare this story to a poem by Dan Pagis:

HARVESTS

The cunning field mouse
Hoards and hoards for years for siege and
    battle,
His winding burrow is full of grain.
Above him

The fire revels in the wheat,
  and in the heart of the sun
Waiting for him, precise and sharp-eyed, the
falcon.

These are different authors writing in different genres, but the sharp, penetrating irony is the same.

Despite the clear parallels between Tchernichovsky's stories for children and his stories for adults, the children's literature is not a simplified, dumbed down version of the adult stories. It is a high-quality fiction that recognizes the possibilities and the limitations of the medium. It refuses to regard the audience—the children—as incomplete adults. Tchernichovsky's children's fiction treats the child with respect and responsibility, and yet it possesses distinct poetic qualities.

WHAT DIDN'T YOU DO IN SCHOOL TODAY, NAUGHTY BOY OF MINE?

The song "Little Jonathan"
A New Reading of an Old Children's Song

There is more in "Little Jonathan" than meets the eye. This familiar, classic children's song deserves a closer analysis. True, the poetic complexity of this ditty does not resemble a Shakespearean sonnet or a poem by Bialik, but it is not as simplistic as you might think, and I will attempt to prove it.

LITTLE JONATHAN

Ran to the garden in the morning
He climbed up a tree
Looking for chicks
Woe to the naughty boy
There's a big hole in his pants
He fell from the tree
And got his comeuppance
        [Lyrics by Israel Dushman]

Reading the text lengthwise, and interpreting it according to the sequence of events from beginning to end will enable us to better discern the dynamics that inform the text.

Here are a few comments about the dynamics of literary textual continuum. These are familiar arguments, but they are worth repeating, especially in regard to this specific text. (1)

In his book *Laoocon* (1766), Gotthold Ephraim Lessing makes a clear distinction between temporal and spatial arts (arts of the dynamic medium versus arts of the static medium), noting that literature is a time-related art form. Indeed, all kinds of texts (but here we focus on literary texts) are based on a continuum of elements (words, sentences, paragraphs, chapters) arranged and spread one after the other, from the beginning of the text to its end. Thus, the reception of the text happens along a stretch of time. Since the elements come in sequence, there is always "earlier" and "later" in the text, not necessarily in the chronology of the events of the plot, but in the temporal relationship existing among elements accumulated one after the other. Some elements are revealed earlier and some are revealed later.

The natural inclination of the reader is to absorb the unfolding information gradually, stage by stage. The reader comes across a distinct piece of information (word, phrase, paragraph, etc.), receives it at first glance, then "digests" it by summing up the qualities and significance of the absorbed information, then continues on, to the next piece of information. It is a piecemeal process, even if the reader is not aware of the fact. Menahem Perry called this process of absorbing and digesting fragmentary textual information "giving a headline."

The typographical quality of a poetic text (short lines, arranged in layers, one under the other) determines and modifies to a certain extent this process of giving a head-line. The reader reads the first line, absorbs and digests its meaning, then moves on to the following line. This consti-tutes the literary phenomena of the dynamics of a literary text. All information is contextual. Thus, no given piece on the textual continuum is complete in and of itself. The complete meaning will be revealed only when the entire context is revealed. Quite often, relatively late information on the continuum "releases" new information, which not only increases the given information, but also sheds light, retroactively, on the way earlier information was perceived.

Thus, the reader is obligated to "read backwards," to go back to the earlier headline and revise it. Sometimes the updating is merely 'cosmetic' and sometimes it is goes much deeper; sometimes it requires total overhauling of the earlier information. A good example is the short story

"The Necklace" by Guy de Maupassant in which the denouement "releases" information that completely and dramatically changes our earlier understanding of the text and dictates a new process of reading-absorption. The earlier text is re-examined in light of the newer, later information. The textual dynamics in "Little Jonathan" is less dramatic and less surprising, but it is no less effective, or perhaps less shrewd.

The opening line is simply "Little Jonathan;" the information is minimal and slim.

And yet two pieces of information are supplied: the protagonist's name and his age. His name is Jonathan and he is "little." We don't find out how little he is until the next line, where we see the child running (presumably) to kindergarten, which would set his estimated age at four or five. Thus, he is a little child, which endears him to the reader. There are also Biblical associations connected to the name Jonathan, since the Biblical Jonathan is a sympathetic, heroic figure. Thus, despite the paucity of information in the first line, there is enough to evoke a positive "headline" in the reader's mind toward Jonathan. The kid, we learn further, "is running in the morning," suggesting that he is an energetic urban child.

Jonathan's destination is somewhat ambiguous: "*gan*" in Hebrew can indicate kindergarten, playschool (reinforcing his young age) or playground, public park, which has implications for the interpretation: if Jonathan is running to kindergarten, our earlier assumption about him is that he is a small, agreeable child, happily running toward an educational facility. But if he is running to a playground—instead of to school—he is not such a model kid, but a mischievous, naughty boy playing hooky, who betrays the trust put in him. If the second option is the correct one, then we have to revise and update the previous headline. Jonathan exhibits some previously unobserved behavioral flaw. The reader expects the ambiguity to be resolved with the provision of further information. The process of reading becomes more accelerated and dynamic.

The reader's expectations for new information that will resolve the ambiguity are met in the following line: "He climbed up a tree." True, there can be trees in the yard of a kindergarten, but a tree is more readily associated with a park, a public garden, or a playground. Thus, although the evidence is not ironclad, there is a strong suggestion that the "culpable" option is the more convincing one. Climbing on a tree in a park is not the innocent behavior of an obedient little boy. The positive headline formed at the beginning of the reading process thus needs revising.

Let us stop for a moment to point out that not every reader (not even a sensitive adult) can discern all those textual subtleties. But those subtleties are there in the text. The imagined reader, then, is the ideal reader, one that can decode a text perfectly and is alive to every literary device embedded in the text.

We left Jonathan climbing up a tree, presumably in a park or a playground, which reinforced the supposition that he is a naughty, rascally truant. The next piece of information further corroborates this supposition: "looking for chicks". The chicks in the nest accord much better with a park, a playground, or a boulevard than with a school. Climbing up a tree in search of chicks is certainly not a normative behavior for a young boy. Jonathan, one assumed, must have been warned more than once not to disturb the peace of the hatchlings in the nest. Jonathan, then, is disobedient and rebellious. He plays hooky, betrays the trust of his guardians, and goes after the chicks.

The initial positive view of our protagonist gives way to a more censorious, incriminating view. The next line accelerates the process and hastens its end: "Woe to the naughty boy." Here is a little poetic revolution. Up to this point, the narrator (the speaker) maintained his position as an external, detached reporter; he revealed the plot but kept out of it, without voicing an opinion. Here is a dramatic rhetorical change: no more neutrality and impartiality, but intervention in the plot. The narrator voices an opinion about Little Jonathan. The "incriminating" headline gains force by the narrator's intervention, by his overt authoritative, judgmental intrusion.

The ending further highlights the incriminating, accusatory version. "There is a big hole in his pants..." Veritable tale of crime and punishment! True, there is no specific information linking the climbing and the hole in the pants; also, bear in mind the instructive comments by Perry and Steinberg regarding narrative devices (2).

However, the narrator's intention is clear; he creates the impression that there is a causal link between climbing the tree and the hole in the pants. Of all the potential possibilities, this one is the most logical.

The narrator discards the pretense of objectivity, injects himself into the plot and uses his authority to nudge the reader toward the incriminating interpretation.

This culminates with the accusing narrator encouraging the reader to deduce that the hole in Little Jonathan's pants is a just punishment for his mischievous behavior.

The poem that began with a positive, benign view of Jonathan became more ambiguous, then steadily more incriminating, culminating with his indictment. In the process, the narrator intervenes in the plot and urges the reader to see the hole in the pants as punishment for naughty behavior (a fact that is not necessarily borne by the facts).

The aesthetic sophistication of the text yields another poetic activity, one that is identified with the same thematic systematization and regimented judgment noted earlier.

The narrator refers to Jonathan three times while reporting his exploits: Little Jonathan, he, and naughty boy—quite a lot, considering the paucity of the text. The choice of this or that designation usually indicates a certain intention. Thus, in the Biblical story of the expulsion of Hagar and Ismael (Genesis, 21, 1-21), Ismael is referred to as "the boy," "the child," "his son," and "the slave's son." These appellations reflect various aspects of the same character. God, objectively, first refers to Ismael as "the boy," and then, following Sarah, as "the slave's son" thereby reminding Abraham that Ismael is indeed a slave girl's son and thus must not outshine Isaac, Abraham's eldest son.

The label "the child" is connected to Abraham, who thereby displays paternal love for Ismael, who is no longer technically a child at this point. Sarah, on the other hand, resents and loathes Ismael, especially after spotting him "playing" with Isaac (Ibid, 10). Playing, in a Biblical sense, can have sexual connotation, thus Ismael exhibits sexual maturity, implying a threat to disinherit Isaac and deprive him of his birthright.

Ismael evokes in Sarah strong feelings of resentment and malice, and she refers to him as "the slave's son." Thus, we see here three appellations, three attitudes from indifference to open hostility. As for the poem—here, too, the protagonist is referred to in three different ways by the narrator, "Little Jonathan," "he," "Naughty Boy," each imparting a different feeling toward the child: "Little Jonathan" implies kind regard and warm feelings; "He" sounds indifferent and impassive, and "Naughty Boy" represents the narrator's censorious and accusatory attitude towards the subject of the poem.

Needless to say, nobody sees Jonathan as a delinquent or a hardened felon, or even deprives him of his natural amiability, but in the given context, "Naughty Boy" implies indignation and rebuke (which is, incidentally, its denotation in the *Mishna*).

Thus, we notice change and progression in the narrator's attitude toward Little Jonathan, a systematic thematic dynamics along the continuum of the text. (3)

But there is also a systematic compositional dynamics (4): the changes and progressions in the textual elements are revealed and spread along the text in a receding fashion, starting with approval, transitioning to indifference, and ending with judgmental censoriousness. The recessive movement corresponds to the changing headlines. The text operates simultaneously two poetic systems, two patterns, or parallel paths producing one poetic effect. The two poetic systems produce a doubling effect: the message is echoed and amplified.

Thus, the modest children's song, though not on a par with Shakespearean sonnets or canonic texts, exhibits well-orchestrated poetic sophistication that is sometimes lacking in more prestigious and respected texts. A proper appreciation of the hidden qualities of the poem requires close reading and interpretation, delving into the depth of its layered poetics.

NOTES

1. For analysis of textual continuum and its poetic potential Cf. Wolfgang Iser: *The Reading Process: A Phenomenological Approach*, NLH Vol. 3 (1972) pp. 279-299), and Yair Mazor, "Another Face of the Literature of the *Haskala*, Tel Aviv University, Tel Aviv 1986 pp.23-60.

2. Menacchem Perry and Meir Steinberg, "Ironic View of the King: Narrative Devices in the story of David and Bathsheba—Two Forays into Theory of Prose". Hasifrut A2 (1986), pp.263-292.

3. For the thematic and compositional dynamics on the textual continuum see: Yair Mazor, "Dynamics of Motifs in the Work of S.Y. Agnon," *Dekel—Academic Publications*, Tel Aviv, 1979.

4. Ibid, pp.12-19.

HEBREW CHILDREN'S LITERATURE: IN THE THICKET OF CONFUSION

LEAH GOLDBERG'S POEM "NIGHTTIME FACING THE GILEAD"

"I ask myself, where did my father
Hide his fear? Perhaps in a locked cabinet,
Or some other place out of reach of the children,
Or deep in his heart..."
—Yehuda Amichai, "The Child Is Gone"

The target audience of children's literature dictates and determines one of its most dominant features, that which distinguishes it from other literary systems. Children's literature is the only one called upon to meet the needs of two distinct potential addressees: the child, the formal consumer of the text, and the adult, the informal reader, who typically selects and picks the text for the child, and quite often reads it, or at least directs the child's reading.

The involvement of the adult requires the author to treat the adult as a potential consumer. Thus, the author is obligated to simultaneously address two target audiences, who will react and respond to the text on two completely different levels.

As result, children's literature finds itself in an anomalous situation; it has a "split personality," having to function on two oppositional strata. This is a very challenging task.

Writers use two strategies to overcome this difficulty: they either ignore the needs of the potential adult reader and address the formal reader, the child, exclusively, or they bypass the adult by flattening, dumbing down content, reducing it to a formal, generic outward shell, while making the adult reader the only addressee of the text.

In the first option (abandoning the adult reader) the texts tend to be simplistic, elementary, condescending. This approach seems lacking in respect for the audience, assuming that the child is an "incomplete, half-baked" adult. The result is often un-canonic or sub-canonic texts depicting an idealized world from which adults have been banished and where the adult world is presented in an unflattering light.

In the other option (abandoning the child reader) the appeal to the child functions only as a formal rhetorical-aesthetic framework, an excuse, using the genre of children's literature, in order to reach an adult audience. The medium is children's literature, but the implied narrator and the potential reader are patently adults. Often the ploy of reaching the adult through the medium of children's literature evinces a parodic attitude toward the model borrowed from children's literature.

Many writers of children's literature eschew using either of these extreme strategies, opting for a balanced and controlled compromise: the text addresses simultaneously both the formal and the informal audiences. They compensate for the compromises in aesthetics and ideas by employing structural and rhetorical devices that answer to the specific requirements of the text. The desired compromise signifies not only concession and withdrawal but also a system of compensation that enhances the text. A text that adopts the option of the controlled compromise presents two frameworks, or levels of significance: one "corresponds" with the child, the other with the adult. The two levels are not discrete; they conduct a dialog of parallels, contrast, and reconciliation, and at the same time they send signals and stimuli, on different levels, to two distinct populations.

Understandably, the level that addresses the child is the more "epidermal," closer to the surface of the text, while the one targeting the adult is a structurally deeper one that calls for a closer reading by the capable, conscientious reader.

The link between the two levels can be effected through parallel, conflict, or reconciliation. When there is a conflict between what is transmitted to the child and what is transmitted to the adult, there can be irreconcilable tension between the two readings of the text: the two readings may be both valid, but they cancel each other out. There is an effect of semantic ambivalence, of irresoluble ambiguity, that both perplexes and fascinates the reader. The reader, who naturally seeks one valid interpretation, has to contend with a situation where there are two opposing interpretations, equally valid, vying with each other. This brings to mind Henry James's story "The Turn of the Screw."

This tense textual ambivalence is a result of a delicate balance among all the components of the two competing systems present in the text. The aesthetic dexterity and the control of the medium often exhibited in children's literature help rescue it from the charge of marginality, which is often leveled against it. It is not just for children; it is also for children.

The poem "Nighttime Facing the Gilead" by Leah Goldberg can serve as a "test case," since it embodies the unsolved ambiguity mentioned earlier. Perhaps we can call it "expressive oxymoron."

NIGHTTIME FACING THE GILEAD

The trees are so heavy,
The fruit bends the boughs,
This is the tranquil hour
When children fall asleep.

From the Gilead down to the valley
A tender black lamb comes down,
A ewe bleats and cries in the pen
It is her little lost son.

The lamb will return to its mother's bosom,
Will lie down in the pen and fall asleep
And the ewe will kiss it
And give it a name.

The night hides among the boughs
And the Gileadite prophet
Silently descends into the valley
To watch the children in their sleep.

Even at first glance, before any "close reading" is attempted, it is obvious to the reader that two distinct thematic materials exist along the textual continuum. On the one hand, materials familiar and expected in the context of this genre, namely, a poem for children: a little lamb, a bleating sheep, pen, mother's bosom, as well as silent night and sleeping children. These elements identify the poem as a cradlesong, a lullaby.

On the other hand, an entirely different set of elements is also present here, materials that are not immediately identified with children's literature, such as: heavy fruit that almost threatens the boughs; the strange reaction of the ewe when the lamb gets to the pen - she "will give it a name"; the prophet descending silently to the valley. Add to these the Biblical allusions, both Jewish and Christian, such as the descent of the lamb, evoking the metaphorical lamb descending to the Valley of the Shadow of Death in Psalms 23, and Ezekiel's vision of the dry bones, or the lamb and the pen (manger) which refer to the Christian mythos.

The lamb, the ewe, and the pen are an intersection of two clusters of materials: one typical of children's literature, the other foreign to it. The context of the cradlesong, which is intended for the child, inspires tranquility, comfort, and security. The boughs heavy with fruit betoken sufficiency and abundance; the lost lamb returns to its mother, the prophet Elijah, like a watchful father guards the peaceful children in their sleep.

This "epidermal" level of the poem presents an innocent, imaginary, idyllic reality. But as often happens, such an outward shell of idyllic existence proves brittle and deceptive: underneath it is a hard core of tragedy. Here, too, the outer layer of the poem is not thick enough to camouflage the inner layer, which is much less serene and idyllic.

The heavy branches overladen with fruit, while connoting ripeness and plenty, can also harbor negative connotations. The descent of the lamb into the valley is connected with loss, suggesting the descent into Hades, the underworld, Hell. Note also that the lamb is not white, as convention would have it, but black. [This is not done for rhyme or rhythm, because the word black—*shahor* in Hebrew—could have easily been replaced by the word *tzahor*—white, pure]. It rather brings to mind the expression "black sheep," which reinforces the negative connotations.

The descent into the valley, evoking the descent into Hades (Hell), is linked to the idea of death, which is associated with sleep (the children's sleep). Not that the children are dead; they are asleep, and yet the evocation of death is not far from the image of to the sleeping children. The image in the final stanza further strengthens the connotation of death. The description of the prophet silently descending into the valley to watch over the children in their sleep immediately conjures up the prophet Ezekiel and his descent into the valley where he sees the vision of the dry bones enveloped in their eerie sleep.

The verb used here—*lehezot* (to watch) has the same root as *hazon* (vision), which further reinforces the allusion to the vision of the dry bones. One Biblical allusion highlights another: the black lamb descending to its perdition, which is a reference to Psalms 23. Thus, the profound, underlying layer of the poem existing underneath the serene and peaceful epidermic level subverts that surface tranquil atmosphere and sends messages of loss and death.

Despite the difference between the layer aimed at the child and the layer aimed at the adult, there is no rivalry between them, but rather a dialogue, a negotiation that creates an interaction on the thematic level of the poem. The positive connotations of the surface level (serenity) and the negative connotations of the deeper level (death) are locked in a wrestling match; sometimes the epidermic layer has the upper hand, relegating the deeper layer to the periphery, and sometimes it is the other way around. At other times, the two are mixed and, instead of a scuffle, there is cooperation.

This kind of "thematic pendulum" requires a rhetorical pendulum based on raising expectations, denying and frustrating them, and then rebuilding them anew. When the negative has the upper hand it creates expectations regarding the projected continuation; a reversal in the balance of powers upsets these expectations and undermines those expectations. In other words, there is a meticulous correlation between the thematic and the rhetoric.

In the first stanza, the positive and the negative, the upper and deeper layers, are evenly maintained and intermingled. There is a sense of peace and serenity suggested by the "the tranquil hour/ When children fall asleep" and the abundance suggested by the heavy branches. Yet this very image of overburdened branches can also suggest the opposite sense of oppression and coercion. By the same token, the children's sleep does not convey the exclusive sense of peace and tranquility but also a vague suggestion of death and loss. These connotations gain force later with the introduction of other elements that presage death.

In the second stanza, a thematic change occurs (with rhetorical implications for creating expectations and frustrating them). The positive connotations expressed in the surface layer recede as the negative tone becomes predominant; the black lamb descends to the valley, as if to the netherworld. The valley itself has the connotation of a grave, a place of loss and oblivion (bolstered by the allusion to Psalms 23, where a metaphorical lamb descends into the Valley of Death). The ewe weeping over her lost lamb further reinforces the negative connotations.

In the third stanza, the lost lamb comes back to its mother, receives a kiss and falls asleep in her bosom. The religious-Christian allusions in this image: ewe, lamb, and sheepfold, again corroborates the sense of serenity, immaculateness, innocence. [The image of the lamb originates in the Old Testament and was later attributed to Jesus by John the Baptist (John 1, 29:36)]

The ewe's strange reaction upon reuniting with her lamb ("give it a name") can be interpreted symbolically in terms of rebirth; the return of the lost lamb represents a rebirth, especially in conjunction with the earlier references to Christ and to the vision of the dry bones. Jesus, symbolized by the lamb, was born in a manger. The lost lamb here is being reborn in the sheepfold. Christ is associated with rebirth and resurrection—which is linked also to the Ezekiel's vision of dry bones hinted at in the last stanza. The bestowing of a name, as is done here to the lost and found lamb, is associated in Scripture with creation, birth or re-birth.

In Genesis, Adam gives names to the newly created beasts, which is an act of verbal creation, and is as significant as concrete creation. When a figure in the Bible undergoes a transformative experience, is being reborn, so to speak, it is accompanied by a change of name. Abram becomes Abraham, Sarai becomes Sarah, and Jacob becomes Israel. By giving the lamb a name, the ewe triggers a whole arsenal of Jewish-Christian connotations. The positive impression that was apparent in the epidermic layer is reasserted in the third stanza.

But the pendulum keeps swaying; there is another change in the fourth and final stanza. The negative and the positive join forces as they did in the first stanza. The sleeping children with the image that evokes traditional lullabies—"The night hides among the boughs"—plus the paternal, protective figure of the Prophet Elijah—recreates the sense of peace and serenity. On the other hand, the allusion to the valley filled with dead bones, conjures up the idea of sleep as death. There is something Gothic, creepy, almost surreal in the reference to the night hiding in the trees, and the prophet emerging from the dark into the bone-filled valley. The fourth stanza, then, like the first one, is oxymoronic in its blend of the positive and negative connotations, the outer and inner layers, the calming and the terrifying effects.

Dividing the component materials in the poem into two opposing categories has implications for the unity of the text. The poem uses compensatory strategies to make up for the thematic separation, unifying and harmonizing the text; for instance, the analogy between the prophet and the lamb. In both cases, the valley is associated with losing the way (in the case of the lamb, it actually gets lost; in the case of the prophet, it is a moral-metaphoric loss, represented by the bones that fill the valley).

Another parallel: the lamb rising from the valley is reborn; in his vision, the Prophet Ezekiel sees the people of Israel arising from the Valley being resurrected. Rebirth described as arising from a valley has a long literary tradition. (Cf. Odysseus' Freudian emergence from the Cave of the Cyclops. There is also a link to a sheep, for Odysseus tied himself to the belly of a sheep and, once outside the cave, let go of the fleece, and was so to speak "born" again.

Similarly, Odysseus is "born" when emerging from the Trojan horse after a symbolic siege of nine years.) Another analogy: the lamb represents Christ, whereas the Gileadite prophet Elijah is traditionally associated with the Messiah. In this close analogy between the descending lamb and the descending prophet, negative and positive qualities coalesce: death is inextricably linked to life: the valley is a grave but also a womb (cf. the common metaphoric view of earth as mother) where new life begins.

Another integrative element in the poem has to do with the use of sound and tone: there is extensive use of the consonant D (in the Hebrew words *kvedim, badim, nirdamin, yeladim, Gilead, yarad, avad, yeradem, dumam*), a unifying device that connects the words and focuses attention on the textual significance. Similarly, the circular textual device of beginning and ending the poem with analogous elements (combining the "rival" layers in the first and last stanza) contributes to the unity and cohesion of the text.

From a compositional point of view, from the way the materials are organized and distributed along the textual continuum, another movement can be discerned in the poem. This compositional movement is largely one of plot, which, unlike the horizontal thematic movement, has an ascendant progression, leading toward a climax. This upward movement is seen in the fact that the main thematic materials of the poem accumulate in the last stanza, either directly or indirectly: night, heavy boughs, children sleeping, and the (dual) descent into the valley.

There is a progression toward a climax, a tapering, conical effect toward the denouement. The simultaneous presence of two contradictory movements—a horizontal thematic one and a compositional climbing one—reflects a basic model that lies at the bottom of the poem: a model anchored in contradictory elements that create ambivalence and oxymoron. The outer, epidermic level exhibits serenity and peace and the profound underlying level that offers death and negation, and the two are inextricably bound.

And here we address the message of the poem, which can be formulated in conceptual terms. The layer that addresses the child reader and the deeper layer that addresses the adult reader both document the same reality, yet each offers a different interpretation of reality. The one addressed to the child purports to defend the child against the darker aspects of reality, or at least to delay its appearance. In this respect, the external level is offered not just as peace and tranquility but also as necessary. Serenity and harmony are presented as perfect, complete and absolute. The deeper layer, which sidesteps the child and aims at the adult, makes no attempt to soften, conceal, mislead or delude. It is all about exposure, disclosure, disillusion. It reveals the darker side of life, its fears and anxieties, without make-up and embellishment.

The reality offered to the adult reader is a complex one of irreconcilable opposites, ambivalence, oxymoron and unresolvable tension, an embarrassing truth but also a necessary and fearless truth. The reality presented to the child is a partial truth, its rough edges smoothed and softened.

Though the framework of the poem is a lullaby, it accommodates the contradictory, ambivalent character of the reality it portrays and the fact that behind the façade of tranquility exists a gloomy reality and the specter of death. There are many cradlesongs that exhibit such split reality. This specific poem is particularly impressive in its sophistication and studied complexity. Certainly, it is a poem for children, but at the same time it is a poem for adults: the more sensitive and attentive among them.

Instructions on How to Press the Right Button

"The Laughter Button"
Children's Poems
by Ronny and Shirley Someck

This slim volume exemplifies a trend characteristic of children's literature: the text contains two simultaneous levels: a simple level directed at the formal recipient of the text, the child, and a complex level directed at the informal, implied recipient, the adult who either buys or reads the text to the child. Later, it will become apparent how challenging and sophisticated is the complex, inner level that addresses itself to the adult.

The typical deeper structure, aimed at the adult reader, is the paratactic structure, which is based on a chain (either short or long) of images or phrases that exhibit close reciprocal resemblance. The paratactic structure lacks the inner framework capable of extricating the paratactic continuum from the horizontal trajectory and leading it toward conclusion and completion. Thus, another element needs to be imported into the paratactic continuum in order to effect a conclusion.

The first paratactic structure appears at the beginning of the book and is based on a sequence of "body machines": vision machine, digestion machine, heart machine and muscle machine. These are paratactic elements that are all concrete physical organs. Next on the textual continuum we find the laugh machine, which differs from the previous ones:

> There is a machine
> That has no fixed site
> It is beloved by all kids, even by Shock-headed Peter
> It is hidden deep inside the body
> And is called
> The laugh machine.

Unlike the other machines, this one is not connected to any part of the body and is, in fact, completely abstract.

The laugh machine, then, is the foreign element that is imposed on the horizontal paratactic continuum propelling it toward its conclusion. The different nature of the laugh machine sets it apart from the other body machines that precede it: it lends it special stature, underlying its prominent position in the narrative of the book. Unlike the other machines, the laugh machine is operated by external stimuli that are not 'trapped' inside the body:

> Sometimes it acts by itself
> When you hear a joke
> Or when you see a bunny
> Disguised as a girl.

And also,

> *Once, when Mom took off her shoes*
> *Shirley slipped her feet*
> *Inside them*
> *She barely made it*
> *To the door*
> *And Mom smiled and said,*
> *"Hey, fancy lady!"*

And later,

> *You can make the dolls laugh*
> *If you paint a bird*
> *And color its face*
> *And its beak red.*

The laugh machine is not triggered by external stimuli (it can be activated by a joke, by a bunny disguised as a girl, or by putting on mom's shoes) and it can cause others to laugh: the dolls laugh, and the doll Ora is funny when her head twists off.

> *But sometimes you laugh*
> *Without any reason*
> *So let's see how to operate this machine.*

You touch various spots on the body: head, nose, cheek and mostly the armpit. Thus, the paratactic structure dictates the thematic development of the plot: the plot focuses on the various ways the laugh machine works, and together they constitute the foreign, external element that deviates from the paratactic order in which the other bodily machines operate. Towards the conclusion of the plot another paratactic structure emerges: Unlike the machines of the body that operate undisturbed and are unlimited, the laugh machine is liable to stop working. Then the question arises: "What do you do if the button [the laugh button] doesn't work?" Various reasons are offered:

> *"Maybe the machine is tired and wants to sit*
> *down or rest?*
> *Maybe the machine is broken and can't move?*
> *Maybe it has a headache?*
> *Maybe it just forgot to count one, two, three?"*

The sequence of questions posed by an anonymous, unidentified entity is soon followed by a question by a well - identified entity: "Once, we could not figure out what had happened and Mom said, Maybe the battery is dead?" The mother's question reignites the laugh machine: "What battery, said Shirley laughing/ This is not a regular machine." And soon afterwards, "Battery is a funny word/ And Shirley's laughter turned the machine back on." The fact that the laugh machine can stop functioning is the foreign element that is imposed on the paratactic sequence (of body machines that do not stop working) and therefore gains special attention. But this 'pessimistic' ending is superseded by the optimistic ending of the book,

At night, when you see a lovely smile
Drawn on the lips
You know that the Machine
Never goes to sleep.

Thus, the book achieves two purposes: stressing the uniqueness of the laugh machine and a promise that it never sleeps.

The poetic sophistication of the book is aimed primarily at the adult reader, the unofficial addressee of the book. But the child, the official addressee, is not ignored: s/he learns about one of the best apparatuses of the body: laughter. Laughter does not operate like the other machines of the body, but it endows the body with a unique and essential quality.

Ronny Someck is fond of telling the following story: A farmer goes home after his day's work. On the way he buys a loaf of bread and a flower. As soon as he gets home, his wife greets him gruffly: Why did you buy a flower? For that kind of money you could have bought another loaf. The farmer says, "The bread I bought so we could live, and the flower I bought so there will a reason to live. The message of "The Laugh Button" aimed at the child, through the mediation of the adult, is that the laugh machine is like the flower in the tale. Laughter does not operate the other machines of the body, but it gives them quality and flavor without which the body machines are sterile. (1)

A TALE OF TWO MONKEYS

"Monkey Tough, Monkey Bluff" by Shirley and Ronny Someck

At the opening of the story, we are introduced to the two main characters:

> *In the heart of the jungle, near Monkey Slough*
> *Lived the twin brothers Tough and Bluff.*
> *Tough was agile, swift and bold*
> *Hung up from trees and played with balls*
> *Bluff spoke in rhymes and liked to snooze*
> *He didn't always tell the truth.*
> *Whenever Bluff lied or misbehaved*
> *His brother always came to his aid.*

The difference in personality and behavior between the two brothers is very clear-cut.

Tough is the "responsible adult" while Bluff is the naughty, mischievous one, always caught in lies and pranks waiting for his clever brother to bail him out. But in fact, the initial description of Bluff anticipates a pattern of reversals and shattered expectations. It includes a reference to Bluff fondness for speaking in rhymes, which encourages the reader—that is, the adult reader, the informal addressee of the text—to harbor some positive expectations of Bluff: he likes to rhyme, meaning he has artistic tendencies. On the other hand, the rest of his description negates those positive expectations: Bluff gets entangled in lies, hanky-panky and annoyances.

And yet the message aimed at the child reader, the formal addressee of the text is clearly a positive one: there is fraternal love, loyalty and devotion between the twins.

The child's point of view is represented in the description of the habitat of the monkeys and the other animals as "a zoo without cages or fences". A child may not be familiar with the concept of a jungle, but surely knows what a zoo is. As in the majority of stories and poems for children, the animals are anthropomorphized (sometimes inanimate objects like rocks, boulders, rain and tears are also humanized). Here we have another device based on suspension of disbelief: all the beasts, predator and prey alike, live peacefully and amicably together. Thus, for example, they buy food and sweets in the supermarket of Michal the Giraffe, carrots in the store of Stephen the Rabbit; they all go to the Jung Cinema to watch movies together.

During the screening of *Tarzan of the Apes*, the monkey Bluff teases the other apes and bamboozles them. This underlines his negative personality: he deceives the other apes and mocks them, taking advantage of their naiveté. His behavior is meant to look reprehensible. However, here the narrator sides with the other apes: while Bluff mocks their supposed cowardice (they are not cowards), the narrator mocks Bluff's own lack of courage:

> *In fact it's Bluff who's faint of heart*
> *Afraid of balls that bounce around*
> *Or drop from tree tops to the ground.*

Here, once more, the brother's twin comes to the rescue:

> *"We must put an end to this," Tough thought*
> *And tried to teach his twin how to cope.*

But to no avail:

> *Bluff could not overcome his dread*
> *Didn't know how to jump or use his hands.*

But here both child and adult readers are in for some un-fulfilled expectations: Bluff learns to kick so well, "his feet became enamored of the balls." He becomes the "King of Goals". But no sooner does he acquire this skill then he is back to the lies and shenanigans. When asked how come he plays ball so well, he puffs up with pride and brags that he was a great kicker already in his mother's womb. He elaborates and embroiders:

> *They called me 'Center-forward fetus'*
> *with golden head and magic feet,*
> *With every kick I scored a goal*
> *The net shook like a leaf in fall*
> *Oh, how I kicked that soccer ball.*
>
> *Yes, training leaves you drained and beat*
> *But I was king of the soccer field.*

This sequence is full of allusions that only a grown-up can identify. The nickname "golden head" is associated with the Israeli soccer player Nahum Stelmach. The phrase "the net shook like a leaf" imitates flowery phrases used by Israeli sports commentators, and the expression, "training leaves you drained" echoes the language of basic training for soccer players. The idea of the fetus kicking in the womb evokes the image of the twins Jacob and Esau fighting in their mother Rebecca's womb.

Another pattern of thwarted expectations emerges: while earlier Tough was critical and disapproving of his brother's fibs, now he reacts enthusiastically to his brother's tall stories, crying, "Hey bro, you're awesome!" This is also anchored in the Israeli culture:

> The use of "bro" is common among soldiers of the Israeli army (IDF). Moreover, the repeated use of the device of thwarted expectations endows the text with a surprising dynamic quality and triggers the reader's interest.

Thus, Bluff continues spreading lies and playing tricks:

> When Bluff was bored he would harass others;
> He would tie the tails of tiger cubs when they
>   were asleep
> And when they woke up, he frightened them
> Saying the tails would remain forever tied."

Here Tough resumes his role of responsible sibling and unties the joined tails. Then, in another incident, Bluff tells the bear that the Kangaroo's pouch is filled with honey. Again, Tough comes to his brother's rescue: he warns the bear of his brother's deceitfulness.

But Bluff does not quit: deception and trickery are second nature to him. He pulls the zebra's leg telling him he ought to buy new clothes, because it is unseemly to walk around in pajamas all day; he sends Michal the Giraffe to Dr. Rhino to have her neck shortened; he tells Leo the lion that the gazelle is plotting to steal his crown; he tells the crow with the grating voice that he was born to sing and therefore ought to study voice with Johnnie the Fox." Here the text is reverting to the adult reader, since the link between the singing crow and the fox is a reference to the famous fable about the sly fox who sweet talks the silly crow into opening his mouth to sing, thus dropping the cheese into the fox's mouth.

But there comes a point when the animals are fed up with Bluff's shenanigans. They call a meeting and brainstorm. In the end Leo the lion comes up with the idea to invite Tough and Bluff to a party at Jung Cinema. When the animals want to know what will happen at the party, Leo says, "It's a surprise."

The following day, when the animals are gathered at the cinema, Bluff is back to his old tricks. When asked where the party is, Bluff denies that there is a party.

Tough arrives at the right moment and reminds the animals about his twin's penchant for fibbing. "The animals went in, ate popcorn and peanuts, and popped some balloons. Suddenly the lion roared, "Ladies and gentlemen, dear animals, please take your seats. The show is about to begin."

The first act is magic tricks performed by two rabbits who charm everyone with their sleight of hand: they whip out doves from a hat, spit fire and swallow swords. Then they announce, 'We need a volunteer to get into a box.' Bluff is quick to volunteer and soon finds himself inside a box, which the magician locks from the outside. Waving a saw, he announces: 'Now we'll saw the box in the middle, and Bluff will only be a half-monkey.' The animals, who have long suffered from Bluff's lies and manipulations, consent enthusiastically. Bluff finally realizes the predicament he is in. He panics and pleads and begs and promises to mend his ways, but his victims refuse to believe him.

This is reminiscent of the story about the boy who cried "Wolf," too often and ended up being abandoned by the villagers when a real wolf attacked his flock. Because of Bluff's chronic lying, nobody believes him that he will never lie again, and he is left trapped in the box. And once again, his twin Tough comes to his rescue. He declares that he trusts Bluff to never lie again, and Bluff is released.

And here the device of thwarted expectations is used once again: the reader is led to believe that after his humiliating experience Bluff is never going to lie again, but this belief is misplaced. When a crying trembling Bluff comes out of the box, Leo the lion asks him to spell the world Truth. Bluff, giving in to his tendency to lie, misspells the word Truth. But unexpectedly, instead of scolding him for lying again, the lion says, "Don't worry, Bluff, you will continue to be an amazing monkey."

One by one, the animals come and hug Bluff, even though he failed in his promise to tell the truth. The message aimed at the child is a message of acceptance and reconciliation: you can forgive people despite their short-comings and failures; you must accept them as they are with their good and bad features.

Bluff's faults do not cloud his achievements: he can still rhyme and excel at soccer; when he lies and pulls a prank, he does not mean to hurt, just wants to have fun. Thus, even though someone has unquestionable faults, we'll do well to remember that that person also has merits, especially when the faults and the naughty behavior are not motivated by malice.

NOTE

1. Shirley Someck is Ronny Someck's daughter. They wrote the book together when she was a little girl.

TWO ADDITIONAL INTRODUCTORY COMMENTS

Two Leading Trends in Children's Literature

We pointed out earlier that children's literature addresses simultaneously two different target audiences: the formal audience, the child, and the informal audience, the adult who picks, buys and perhaps reads the book to the child. The address to the child is twofold: drawing the child's attention to the action (in the story or the poem) and directing the child's attention to the pedagogical-educational message represented by the plot and by the characters in the text. Adult mediation is required to guide and direct the child so s/he can discern, understand and internalize the "hidden" pedagogical message embedded in the text.

And another comment: many children's stories (and often poems) are based on a quest, on a journey of discovery carried out by the protagonist in an attempt to unravel a mystery. Yakova Sacredoti, a scholar of children's literature, calls this journey "crusade". It can also be seen as an Odyssey, modeled after the Homeric quest. The protagonist sets out on a journey of discovery that is conducted in stages, and culminates in the finding of a truth that is very significant. Locating and exposing the hidden truth mark the conclusion of the story or the poem and are accompanied by a lesson or moral. This is the pedagogical core of the text: imparting insight that will affect the child's relation to reality. Moreover, quite often, the gradual progression of the Odyssean quest creates a paratactic structure based on an accumulation of elements that display mutual similarity. The paratactic sequence has no inner structure that can propel it toward a conclusion; therefore an exterior element, foreign to the paratactic continuum, is needed to impose itself on the horizontal continuum and navigate it toward the ending. This, naturally, involves an element of surprise, and surprise invests the textual continuum with originality, dynamism, and allure.

A SISTER FOR SALE
The Story "A Feeling for Business" by Nurit Zarchi

The story is based on a literary-Biblical motif: envy of older siblings toward their younger, more successful ones. Young David evoked the envy of his older brothers (especially the eldest, Eliav): God rejected them as candidates for the throne, and the prophet Samuel anointed young David as king in the presence of his siblings who looked on resentfully and enviously. Indeed, when their father Yishai sent David to inquire after his brothers, who had followed King Saul in the battle against the Philistines, Eliav, seething with rage, scolded and reprimanded him, even though David was merely carrying out their father's instructions. Joseph's brothers envy their young, clever brother who is their father Jacob's favorite.

In our story, the older sister (who is seven years old) is envious of her young sister (who is about four). When the older girl hears that their father had to declare bankruptcy, she tries to sell her sister. There is an echo here to the story of Joseph and his brothers. The jealous brothers, who resent and detest Joseph, sell him to a caravan of Ishmaelite merchants on their way to Egypt, where he is later sold into slavery.

It is quite possible that the child reader is not familiar with the Biblical story of Joseph and his brothers, or with the story about David and his brothers. At this stage, it is the adult reader's decision to choose at what point to bring up the Biblical allusions and explain their relevance to the story.

From the very beginning, the reader is made aware of the envy that the older sister, Ma'yan, feels toward her well-liked, successful younger sister, Oshrit,

> *Everybody's always saying how pretty Oshrit is, how sweet, graceful and talented. And her behavior is so exemplary. She's playing Lego now. She's never lost a single brick since the day she got it.*

Indeed, Oshrit is perfect. Ma'yan, on the other hand,

> *"What do I do? I sit behind the screen, where no one can see me, and I hear Dad telling Mom,*

"Nothing doing. I'm afraid I'll have to declare bankruptcy.'"

In other words, while Oshrit is a model child, Ma'yan is a snoop. She eavesdrops on the grown-ups' conversations. Joseph, it will be remembered, (falsely) accused his brothers of spying when they came to Egypt trying to buy food during a famine. (In fact, Joseph himself used to spy on his brothers in his youth.)

The Biblical allusion to spying is further extended. Ma'yan reports that she sees Oshrit pointing her eyes not in the direction of Mom and Dad, but to the middle of the room. This is her routine, so as not to appear to spy on them. Biblical Joseph, too, used to report to his father about his older brothers, slandering them behind their backs.

Ma'yan's mother explains that bankruptcy means shortage of money. Ma'yan boasts that she has her father's knack for business (at least he had it until now). At night she sits down and makes a list of people with whom she could conduct business to generate money. Here is the list:

1) Ovadia Toimalo—the family's domestic help, who hails from faraway Africa.

2) Mr. Hirosiki - a Japanese businessman with whom Ma'yan's father conducts business.

3) The supermarket manager, who always calls Oshrit "Cutie pie" and "little angel," whereas about Ma'yan, he says, "the kid's really growing." The different comments stoke the older girl's resentment and envy of her sister.

4) The girls' ballet teacher (despite Oshrit's young age, her dancing talent allowed her to join an advanced class).

5) The commercial secretary who visits the father before his trip to America.

6) Kobi, the father's younger brother, who lives in Germany but comes frequently for visits. "When he arrives, he always pats Oshrit, telling her how cute she is and how devoted he is to the girls. He wishes he had a sweet girl like her."

Ma'yan hopes that at least one of these people will agree to do business with her, so she could make some money. And here comes the punch line: All these people will surely want to buy Oshrit, since she is "the most precious thing in our family." Thus, Ma'yan hopes to kill two birds with one stone: help her father in his failing business, and get rid of her little sister, the object of her envy.

This punch line is naturally a surprise. The surprise underlines the impractical and immoral nature of this 'business venture." At least Joseph's sale by his brothers, though it was immoral, was practical. Ma'yan's plan is much worse.

From now on, Ma'yan sets out on a quest that brings to mind Odysseus' voyage of discovery in Greek mythology. She goes from one person to another, hoping to make a deal for the sale of her younger sister. Each of them (including the ballet teacher) reacts differently to her business initiative, but all of them adamantly refuse. Her father's Japanese business partner smiles benignly but turns her down. Ovadia has many children of his own; he likes Oshrit but is not interested in having another daughter. The idea itself arouses in him longings for his children and sorrow for their separation. The ballet teacher, Ms. Juta Wanchansky, reacts with annoyance and anger. Uncle Kobi back from Germany is vehemently opposed to the idea: "God forbid! Nobody should do such things!" The transition from person to person, from one negative reaction to the next, creates a paratactic structure, a continuum of accumulating elements of similar nature. This is a horizontal continuum with no internal element that can resolve it and lead it to a denouement.

The paratactic continuum is based on successive failed attempts to reach a deal (the sale of Oshrit). An external element is, therefore, required to interrupt the sequence and bring it to a halt. The encounter with Mr. Yehuda, the manager of the Supermarket serves as that external element. When Ma'yan encounters Mr. Yehuda, she says to herself, "I will tell him everything." The reader assumes that Ma'yan is about to offer Oshrit to Mr. Yehuda, but this expectation is frustrated; instead of trying to sell her sister to him, she tells him about her father's bankruptcy.

This puts an end to the paratactic structure, and the story acquires a new trajectory, focusing on the girls' paternal grandmother and her son Kobi who has come for a visit. It is obvious that Grandma is not pleased with her younger son, who often proves opinionated and insensitive. The focus on the grandmother and the uncle from Germany leads to a new business avenue. The mother, in an attempt to generate some money, sells the precious ornate Biedermeier furniture that the family had inherited to a dealer in Jaffa, and she buys instead some modern, much cheaper furniture. The dealer drives Ma'yan to his exotic old furniture store in Jaffa and asks her to keep an eye on the store for a moment. Ma'yan feels like a mature and responsible businesswoman, but when the dealer does not return until dark, her self- confidence evaporates. Only later that night, when the tired and hungry girl is left alone with her father, does she confess to him all her business initiatives. The father reprimands her, but he does so pleasantly and sympathetically.

Throughout the story, the impression one gets of Oshrit, the younger sister, is of a sweet and innocent girl, totally oblivious to her older sister's scheming and conniving. But this is not really the case. At the beginning of the story, Ma'yan notes that Oshrit does not look straight at her parents, only to the center of the room. She does not want to seem to be spying. Thus, it is not only the older sister who snoops (hiding behind a screen and eavesdropping on her parents' conversation); the little sister who seems so sweet and helpless does that, too.

A girl in the ballet class says to Ma'yan, "You don't have to love somebody." Oshrit interjects, "So what if you don't love somebody?" Presumably, she refers to her relations with her older sister, and her comment sounds clever and mature.

When Ma'yan comes back disappointed from her failed attempt to sell Oshrit to the ballet instructor, Oshrit accompanies her, "and in order to annoy her, Oshrit hums a tune softly all the way home." Sweet little Oshrit is not so guileless. She riles her older sister and taunts her.

When the sisters argue, Oshrit says, "if it doesn't suit you that I have things to say, too, then go to Germany."

Oshrit may be cute and sweet, but she is not naïve or helpless. When Ma'yan tries to hide from her mother the fact of her disappearance in the furniture store in Jaffa, "Oshrit came and looked me in the eye." She can be wily and not always kind. When Ma'yan asks her to turn down the TV or to change channels, Oshrit ignores her. The mother scolds Ma'yan, and "Oshrit looked me straight in the eye and said, 'Poor Ma'yan.'" The angelic kid sure knows how to tease and taunt, and not always without malice.

What, then, is the pedagogical message the text means to convey to young readers?

Life is not black and white. Ma'yan is wrong and should be criticized for trying to sell her little sister, but she also deserves our sympathy and understanding; after all, she was trying to help her family when they were in financial straits. Oshrit is indeed cute and well behaved, but she is not guileless, and she can be a little mean. This book is not just about Ma'yan and Oshrit: it is about relationships between siblings. It is a book about life and about people.

THE VOYAGE TO MATURITY

The Story "Morning Star" by Michal Snunit

Like "A Feeling for Business," which is based on a Biblical allusion (the story of Joseph and his brothers), "Morning Star," too, is based on a literary allusion, this time to Greek mythology. The reference is to the story of Narcissus and Echo. The goddess Hera punished Echo, dooming her to a love that can never be realized. Echo falls in love with Narcissus, the son of the Nymph Lyriope, but he spurns her and ignores her pleas. Artemis, the goddess of hunt, punished Narcissus for his vanity and condemned him to a life of unfulfilled love. One day, passing by a clear fountain, Narcissus saw his image reflected in the water and fell in love with it. Tortured by the inability to possess the object of his infatuation, he died of longing and agony.

The fundamental allusion here to the story of Narcissus is complex; parts of it deviate from the classical mythological version, giving the story multifaceted qualities and a special appeal.

The main character of the story is a young girl named Morning Star (*Ayelet Hashahar*). She was as pretty as the eponymous planet, and it was rumored that she was born of the stars. Her loneliness and isolation are stressed. Mythological Narcissus had parents, but he was also very lonely, vaingloriously pushing away all those who sought his company. Morning Star, too, rejects the advances of the handsome boy who wants to befriend her. But one thing causes Morning Star acute sorrow. Whenever she gazes at the river, all she can see is the sky and the stars reflected in the water, but she can never see her own image. This is a direct reference to Narcissus who fell in love with his own reflection in the fountain.

True, the details of the two stories are not identical, but this lends the story its originality and charm. The fact that Morning Star is unable to see her own reflection causes her tremendous pain. The reason for this inability to see herself is that instead of eyes she has two stars.

Thus, Morning Star sets on an Odyssean voyage of discovery, hoping to find remedy for her deficiency. She hears about an old woman who lives in a distant forest, perhaps a good fairy, perhaps a witch, and decides to seek her out. She finds the forest and the old lady, who turns out to be a good fairy. But unfortunately, she cannot help Morning Star. She can, however, weave magical scarves from spider webs that play musical tunes. She weaves one such scarf for Morning Star, and the girl puts it on and makes her way to the next station on her quest.

Next, she pays a visit to a giant who is either kind or mean; she does not know beforehand, but decides to visit him anyway. Luckily, he turns out to be a kind-hearted giant, but he, too, cannot not help her. He tells her, "All I can do is mix colors to make bright ribbons that tell stories." The kindly giant concocts a gorgeous ribbon for her that he ties to her hair to adorn her, and the ribbon tells her comforting stories. She thanks him and continues on her odyssey.

Her next stop is a magical bird. Unlike the earlier stations in which she did not know beforehand whether the fairy or the giant were benevolent beings, we are told in this case that the magical bird is a friendly one. In this respect the third station functions as the element that disrupts the paratactic path and leads it toward its conclusion. Indeed, the bird is marvelous beyond belief, but she, too, is incapable of helping Morning Star. Instead, she weaves her a magic carpet, a flying carpet that can take its owner straight home. Unlike the earlier visits, the bird helps Morning Star with a piece of advice. "Don't look for help in faraway places; only you can help yourself," she says cryptically.

> So Morning Star sat
> On the flying carpet
> The scarf around her neck,
> The ribbon in her hair
> Flying home.
> But she hardly remembered
> The bird's wise words.

Time passes. Morning Star found solace in the musical scarf and the colorful ribbon that told her stories, and in the magic carpet that brought her home every time she flew away. But she remained unhappy because she was still unable to see her reflection in the river. She forgot what the magical bird had told her: that she need not look for a solution far away but in herself. She did not realize that the flying carpet was an embodiment of that sage advice, since it always brought her home.

One day, when bending to look at the water, she saw a reflection of a boy in the river. Alarmed, she turned her head and saw a young man standing on a rock. The boy saw her lovely reflection in the water and smiled at her. But Morning Star was taken aback, ignored him, and then told him to go away. This echoes the Narcissus story: he also alienated everyone who sought his company, and was especially dismissive of Echo. But the boy was not deterred; he came every day, stood on the rock, and watched his own reflection in the water, next to that of lovely Morning Star. She, on her part, vigorously roiled the water to erase his likeness.

One day, she came to the river and noticed that there was no one on the rock. The boy who so adored her, despaired of her rejection and went away. Thereupon, a dramatic change took place in Morning Star's feelings and personality. The rejected boy's absence made her realize how hopelessly lonely she was. For the first time in her life, she experienced the deep agony of loss. The protective fence around her began to crumble. She felt the loss of a close person. Morning Star burst out crying and covered her face with her hands. She wept for a long time, mourning the loss of a man who was in love with her, and only now did she realize that she loved him, too. As she bent down to wash her tearful face in the river, to her utter surprise, for the first time in her life, she saw her reflection in the water.

Breaking the circle of loneliness, needing a loving soul in her life, distancing herself from the myth of Narcissus—

all led to overcoming her blindness, to an ability to remove the layer that shielded her eyes and to see herself as she really is.

The message for the young reader is this: loneliness puts a distance between the world and us. Our willingness to welcome loving people into our lives enables us to understand ourselves realistically, bravely, and effectively. Like most children's stories, Morning Star, too, has a "happy ending." As soon as the heroine sees her reflection in the river, she starts looking for the loving and beloved boy. She eventually finds him in the forest, tells him about her past, about her sorrow and confesses her love for him. The flying carpet brings them to the river, where they see both their images reflected in the water, and are greatly moved. Morning Star finally understands what the magic bird has told her. Only she can cure herself of her blindness and of her grief. As soon as she abandons her narcissistic desire to reject those who seek her company—including the one who loves her—then her heart opens up to receive another into her life and her eyes are opened.

This is a story about an odyssey into the depth of a girl's psyche, where her soul is besieged and imprisoned. It is a journey of initiation that, like archeological excavation, unearths her maturity from underneath layers of childishness that kept her besieged behind a fence of loneliness. This is her voyage to maturity; the deep and real happy end is her ability to break away from the constricting fence she has erected around herself and open herself to the world.

LEAH GOLDBERG
INTRODUCTORY COMMENT

Leah Goldberg (b. 1911 Germany–d. 1970 Jerusalem) was one of the most prominent writers of Modern Hebrew Literature. She was poet, fiction writer, playwright, translator, children's literature writer, and professor of comparative literature at the Hebrew University in Jerusalem. In all these areas of creativity, she exhibited originality and was very prolific; her works have become classics of Modern Hebrew Literature. Her first book of poems, "Smoke Rings," was published in 1935. Her second book, "Green-eyed Ear of Corn," was published in 1940. During those years and in years to come, she published many poems and stories for children.

Her poetry was influenced by Russian symbolism, and yet she tried to distance herself from the formalistic-sensual as well as the metaphorical aspects of that movement, and to focus instead on intellectual, analytical layers with clearer content. Her poems deal with individualistic, rather than national or universal themes; they focus on lost love, the disappointments of love, feelings of guilt, and the longing for the European landscapes she left behind. Among her translations of world literature, of particular note are Tolstoy's "War and Peace," short stories by Chekhov, as well as works by Shakespeare, Ibsen, Petrarch, and others.

Yair Mazor

Guess Who's Coming to Stay
The Story "A Flat for Rent" by Leah Goldberg

This is the first in a series of three stories that appeared in one book. This story (and perhaps this is the reason for publishing the three together) has a distinct paratactic structure. The story is a series of narratives (sub-stories) that have distinct similarities. They form a horizontal continuity, which is devoid of an internal mechanism that can lead toward a conclusion. Thus, an external element, foreign to the thematic portrait of the continuum, is called for in order to disrupt the horizontal progression and bring on a denouement.

The story opens thus:

> *In a beautiful valley, among vineyards and fields, stood a five-story tower. Who lives in this tower? On the first floor lives a fat hen. All day long she tosses and turns in her bed. She is so fat she can hardly walk. On the second floor lives a cuckoo bird. All day long she runs around, paying visits, since her children live in other homes. [At this point the adult reader should explain to the child why the cuckoo's chicks live and grow up in others' nests.] On the third floor lives a black cat, neat and coquettish, with a ribbon around her neck. On the fourth floor lives a squirrel, happily cracking nuts. On the fifth floor lived Mr. Mouse. A week ago he*

packed his belongings and left. Nobody knows
where he went and why.

Since the mouse had left, the tenants hung a sign on the entrance saying, "Flat for Rent." And here begins the paratactic structure of the story: one by one, different animals visit the house to inspect the empty flat. Each visit echoes the one before and, in fact, is almost identical to it. The first one to visit is an ant. The neighbors come to greet her, and this is the dialog that ensues.

Do you like the rooms? they ask, and the ant
says, "The rooms are nice."
"Do you like the kitchen?"
"The kitchen is nice."
"Do you like the hallway?"
"The hallway is nice."
The tenants are pleased and ask, "Will you come
live with us?"
To their great disappointment, the ant declines
the invitation and explains that, as the industri-
ous creature she is, she cannot live in the same
house with a lazy hen, who is so fat she can
barely walk. And the ant goes away.

The second prospective tenant is a rabbit. The same dialog is repeated.
"Do you like the rooms?"
"The rooms are nice."
"Do you like the kitchen?"

"The kitchen is nice."
"Do you like the hallway?"
"The hallway is nice."

Again, the delighted tenants invite her to move in, but again the same rhetorical pattern is repeated and the expectations are thwarted. Even though the rabbit finds the flat comfortable, she refuses to move in.

I don't like the neighbors. How can I, a mother of
twenty bunnies, live with the cuckoo bird who
deserts her children? Her children grow up in
strangers' nests, abandoned and neglected.
What will my children learn from them?

The cuckoo felt slighted, and the rabbit went on her way.

Next, it is the pig's turn. "He stood there; his tiny eyes inspected the walls, the ceiling and the windows. Again the same dialog is repeated between the tenants and the prospective lodger,

"Do you like the rooms?"
"The rooms are nice."
"Do you like the kitchen?"
"The kitchen is nice, even though it is not filthy
enough" [Pigs, after all, like to wallow in muck].

"Do you like the hallway?"
The hallway is nice.

And again, the tenants are disappointed. The pig refuses to rent the flat, arguing, "I don't like the neighbors. How can I, the son of white pigs from time immemorial, live with a black cat? No, this does not suit me at all." The neighbors are hurt and angry and they send the pig on his way.

Next comes a nightingale and the paratactic structure continues on its horizontal trajectory with the familiar dialog. "Do you like the rooms? The rooms are nice. Do you like the kitchen? The kitchen is nice. Then stay with us, said the tenants." But the nightingale, too, refuses.

> *No, I won't. I don't like the neighbors. How can I find peace and quiet with the squirrel cracking nuts all day, making a terrible, ear-splitting ruckus? My ears are accustomed to other sounds, to songs and hymns.*
>
> *The squirrel was offended and the nightingale went on his way.*

Now comes the turn of the dove. Surprisingly, the dialog changes,

> *Do you like the rooms? The rooms are narrow. Do you like the kitchen? It is nice but not roomy enough. Do you like the hallway? There is too much shade. The hallway is dark."*

The paratactic continuum has reached its end with the insertion of a foreign element that disrupts the cumulative progression. The foreign element is the dove, who is the first to find fault with the flat. But here the reader encounters another surprise: even though the dove (unlike her predecessors who praised the flat) finds faults with the flat, she gladly rents it!

The external element that brings about the conclusion is thus twofold. Here the quest comes to an end with the introduction of a redeeming "foreign" element. And what prompted the dove to rent the flat that the other animals rejected? It was the neighbors—the same neighbors that were the reason for the earlier rejections. The dove praises the neighbors.

> *The hen with her pretty comb, the lovely cuckoo*
> *bird, the neat and clean cat, and the nut-*
> *cracking squirrel, so full of zest. I know that we*
> *can all live together in harmony, happily and*
> *peacefully.*

The fact that it is the dove that is willing to live peacefully and harmoniously with the other animals is not accidental. Since the Biblical story of Noah and the flood, the dove has acquired positive connotations and has been associated with peace and reconciliation. However, here, too, an explanation by an adult is required to point out these references to the child reader.

IF YOU DO IT, DO IT RIGHT
The Story "This Way and Not That Way"
by Leah Goldberg

This story, like the previous one—"Flat for Rent"—is conducted in two parallel tracks that echo, reflect and interpret each other. One track progresses along the cumulative paratactic continuum, which eventually is disrupted and diverted towards a resolution.

The second track is an Odyssean quest, which is completed at the end of the horizontal paratactic track. The story is based on a cumulative sequence of thematic images and fragments of plot that exhibit close, reciprocal analogies. What links the disparate parts of the plot is the fact that Little Anat asks her father to draw her a picture that tells a story, such as a dog in a kennel, a man with a moustache reading a newspaper, a cat chasing a little mouse, or a picture of a nice house, a boat in the sea, etc.

But every time the father tries to draw a picture, he destroys the logical order of the reality he paints. Thus, he paints the mustachioed man sitting in the dog's kennel while the dog sits on a chair reading a newspaper; he draws a giant mouse chasing a tiny cat, and a house floating in the sea while the boat is perched on the top of a mountain. The father draws a little girl sleeping underneath a bed, while her shoes and socks lie on the bed. He draws a giant chick laying a hen inside an egg and a man and a woman eating supper, while the silverware is on the chair and the woman is on a plate and the man eats a napkin.

These "stations" on the paratactic continuum have another common denominator: they make Anat laugh. She points out the shattered, distorted reality in all those pictures, and the father agrees with her and redraws the picture, this time in conformity with accepted reality. Except for the last picture: a cart, a child, and a horse, which serves as the external element, outside the paratactic continuum, which forces itself on the sequence and brings about the conclusion.

Anat asks her father to draw a cart, a child, and a horse. Again, the father makes a mistake, painting a picture that ignores normative reality: the child is drawing the cart while the horse sits on his shoulders. But unlike the earlier scenes, this time the father does not correct his mistakes and does not restore the scene to conventional reality. The phone rings, the father puts down the unrealistic picture, hastens to answer the phone and does not return. Thus, the last picture is unlike the earlier ones (which were corrected and made to conform to accepted reality), the sequence is disrupted and the paratactic continuum is brought to a halt.

Interestingly, adults are usually the ones anchored in solid reality while kids tend to daydream and construct an imaginary reality that challenges the norm. In our story, this is reversed; the adult fails to obey the rules of normative reality while the child is the one standing on solid ground. This, then, is the message to the child: You can do it, too. Since the father does not have a chance to correct the mistaken representation, Anat takes it upon herself to draw a new picture that restores the faulty reality in the father's drawing. Thus she draws a child holding the reins while the horse draws the cart.

Here the odyssey comes to an end: the child learns to overcome the limitation of her age, to take the initiative, and to rely on her talents and artistic independence, thus replacing the adult who has "deserted the battlefield" so to speak. The child's drawing may not be as polished and attractive as the adult's, but it is independent and realistic.

This, then, is the pedagogical message the story conveys to the young readers: you can act independently, artistically, and without adult direction or assistance.

THE ROAD TO HAPPINESS
The Story "A Tale of Three Nuts"
by Leah Goldberg

This story, like the two previous ones, has a dual structure: the paratactic structure and the quest, an Odyssey-like structure. Here, too, the paratactic, horizontal structure is disrupted toward the end, when a foreign, alien element forces itself on the cumulative sequence and diverts it from its trajectory toward an ending. The point where the continuum stops marks the end of the Odyssean quest.

The story opens with a squirrel who finds itself homeless when the rainy season comes and the tree where he has resided sheds all its leaves. In distress the squirrel asks a kindly dwarf to let him stay in his house until spring. The dwarf agrees but wants something in return, "Alright, you can stay, but what will you give me in return?" The squirrel answers in rhyme:

> *Three nuts will I provide*
> *With three secrets inside*
> *Whoever cracks their code,*
> *Will be the happiest in the world.*

The dwarf takes the squirrel in, and the squirrel gives him three nuts, one the size of a pea, one the size of an egg, and one as big as a grapefruit. The squirrel tells the dwarf, "Guard these nuts with your life, because one day they may save you."

These are no ordinary nuts
They have great secrets in their hearts
Whoever cracks their code,
Will be the happiest in the world.

When spring comes, the squirrel thanks the dwarf and goes away.

The nuts were hidden in the attic, and the dwarf kept a watchful eye on them.

One morning, the dwarf discovered three men with big axes in the forest. They told him that a noble prince had sent them to cut down all the trees so he could build a magnificent palace for his beloved.

The dwarf pleaded with the axmen, "Spare the trees, spare the birds and the beasts that live in the forest, spare me, helpless little dwarf." And then he made an offer to the three tree-cutters: if they spared the forest, he would give them "The three nuts with/ Great secret in their hearts/ Whoever cracks their code/ Will be the happiest in the world."

The loggers accept the deal: they take the nuts and go to the noble prince who had hired them. The dwarf was elated, danced for joy, and recited these verses:

There once were three nuts
With secrets in their hearts
I cracked their code
And I'm the happiest in the world.

Understandably, the dwarf had reason to celebrate: he saved the trees from extinction. But in what way did he solve the mystery at the center of those nuts? How did he crack their code? This question remains unanswered.

The paratactic sequence—with its concomitant Odyssean quest—now moves to the next station. The three magical nuts are still at the center. The tree-cutters return to the prince and fearfully and servilely reveal that they did not cut down even one tree. The prince is furious. He explains that he has fallen in love with an amazingly beautiful woman and she consented to marry him on condition that he mows down the trees and builds her an incomparably sumptuous palace.

The woodcutters try to placate the prince by telling him, "We brought you a treasure more fabulous than any palace." The prince desires to possess that treasure. "Bring it to me," he orders. But the woodcutters request him to pay each of them two shekels for the treasure. And this is how they present it to the prince,

> Look, here are the three nuts
> With secrets in their hearts
> Whoever cracks their code
> Will be the happiest in the world.

The price gleefully accepts the nuts, pays them two shekels each, and sends them on their way. They go away singing,

There once were three nuts
With secrets in their hearts
Three people cracked the code
And are the happiest in the world.

At this point in the second phase of the paratactic continuum, the same question recurs. The tree cutters have a reason to rejoice: they are relieved of the strenuous work of cutting down the forest and, besides, they were handsomely paid by the prince; but as in the case of the dwarf, you wonder why they sing about having solved the mystery, for the secrets of the nuts remain hidden and inscrutable. There is no answer to this query. The mystery is not solved, and the quest has to continue.

The noble prince convinces his beloved that the magic nuts promise happiness much greater than a palace, however sumptuous. The girl consents to marry the prince, and they are very happy in their union. But the riddle of the magic nuts has not been solved. The paratactic structure is undisturbed and the quest remains a challenge.

The last segment of the story introduces the external narrative unit that disrupts the continuum and propels it toward a conclusion. This narrative segment is different than its predecessors. Here the five-year-old son of the prince and his wife finds the hidden nuts, cracks them and eats their meat with great relish. And this is the heart of the mystery that drives the plot: no secret and no mystery reside in the three nuts. Their special quality consists in the fact that they cause people to do good deeds, and that brings them happiness.

The dwarf saved the squirrel from a deadly winter, and then saved the forest from extinction, and these deeds elate the dwarf and bring him happiness. The prince's servants spare the forest in exchange for the nuts; their happiness leads them to believe that they have discovered the hidden secret of the nuts. The prince and his wife show mercy in sparing the trees and are rewarded with a happy married life.

Thus, the secret of the nuts is that there is no secret, except their ability to spur and inspire people to do good deeds. Thus ends the quest: the secret is revealed. Ironically, it could have been divulged even before the end of the quest.

A NOCTURNAL QUEST

The Story "A Moonless Night"
by Shira Geffen and Etgar Keret

Like many children's stories, "A Moonless Night" progresses along two parallel paths: the horizontal paratactic one and the Odyssean quest that comes to a conclusion at the end of the story. The paratactic structure is based on a dense, dynamic continuum that raises expectations and then thwarts them.

This is a story about disappointment. The moon disappears and Little Zohar goes on a journey to find it. This quest is full of disappointments and frustrated expectations. In fact, the story opens with a frustration. Zohar's father finishes reading a story to her and leaves the room (forgetting to say "Good Night"). Little Zohar calls to him twice, "You forgot to turn on the nightlight." But the father replies, "There is no need for a nightlight tonight, because there is a full moon in the sky."

The unhelpful father leaves the room without bothering to make sure that his words have actually calmed down the frightened little girl. The story ends with another disappointing, deceiving person who monopolizes the moon, and would not let it light the world. The story is cyclical: it opens and concludes with a frustrating, faithless man. Both cases involve the disappearance of the moon.

The disappointing (perhaps deceiving) father's assertion that there is a full moon in the sky proves wrong: there is not even a sliver of a crescent moon. Zohar is a little girl, but she is not without pluck and resourcefulness. Thus, Zohar embarks on an Odyssean quest, looking for the missing moon; she is determined to find the moon and to restore it to its natural place in the sky.

At the first station of her quest, Zohar calls out, "Moon." But then she remembers that the moon has another name, Luna, so she calls out, "Luna," but she is greeted only with silence and darkness. Zohar begins to speculate: Maybe the moon climbed on the roof? Maybe it fell into a well? Maybe it fell asleep on a treetop and never woke up? But these assumptions are soon dismissed. Now Zohar embarks on the second stage of her quest for the missing moon. She notices something shiny on the lawn, something round and big and white. But again she is disappointed: this is not the lost moon, just a fat white cat.

Zohar addresses the cat politely, asking if he knows where the missing moon may be. But the cat, rudely awakened from his sleep answers gruffly,

> "What have I got to do with the missing moon?
> Whatever isn't treat or fare
> Can get lost, for all I care."

And the cat goes back to sleep. But Zohar does not give up; she goes on to the next stage in her quest for the lost moon. She spots a circle of white light, stretches her arms and calls, "Moon!" But to her great disappointment, a deep voice answers from the darkness, "Who's calling there?" It is a policeman who asks Zohar for details of the lost moon. Zohar smiles and says,

> *"Sometimes it's white, sometimes it's yellow,*
> *Sometimes it's small, sometimes it's huge,*
> *Sometimes it's a sliver,*
> *Sometimes it's round,*
> *Sometimes it's old; sometimes it's young*
> *But it is always shining."*

The policeman is irritated and confused by these contradictory attributes, and he tells Zohar to go home. But Zohar is not deterred by this response and is determined to persist in her quest. She continues to walk through the dark streets until the sidewalk ends, and the fences, the cats, the yards, and the benches all end. The streetlamps are turned off and tears stream down Zohar's cheeks.

Suddenly, in the distance, she notices a bright light, as white as ivory and she starts making her way toward it.

It is not easy reach that spot.

> *"In the wood the crickets chirp*
> *Other noises fill the air,*
> *A brown owl with a crooked beak*
> *Cried, 'Kid, go home! Double quick!'*
> *Old cypress trees and pines*
> *Glared at her with angry eyes*

But Zohar didn't give up the fight
And continued to walk toward the light.

Like the earlier stages of the Odyssean quest (with the transition from one station to the next on the paratactic structure), Zohar is bound to be disappointed. Next, she spots a cottage from which a stream of light gushes forth. And here a quick turning point occurs: Zohar knocks on the door several times, until the door opens a crack and a bald head with a frightened face appears.

"Who's knocking on my door?" He cries, "Are you a boy? A Girl? An elf in disguise?"

But as soon as Zohar asks for help, the man's behavior changed. "One must always offer help—I will gladly lend my hand."

But the bald man's help (offering nails, sails, mosquito net, odorless flower, pencil box, multiplication table) proves useless in the quest to find the missing moon. The man finally exclaims, "I have no moon. Go to the neighbors," and slams the door, leaving Zohar upset and frustrated. Once again, hope turns to disappointment. The transition to the next station is particularly dramatic.

Zohar finds out that the bald man has led her astray. He sent her to the neighbors in an attempt to find the moon, but it turns out that there are no neighbors. However, she notices a very long ladder that seems to reach all the way to the sky. She climbs the ladder and soon reaches the next station on her odyssey, the one that brings the quest to a close, and cuts short the paratactic continuum. It is at this station that the missing moon is found.

While climbing the high ladder she peeks through the window of the cottage, and discovers the following amazing scene: the bald man is playing merry tunes while the moon is dancing barefoot on a table.

Zohar is furious: she storms into the cottage and bawls out the bald man:

> *"Liar, cheat, thief of the moon*
> *Selfish man, aren't you ashamed*
> *The sky is dark, there's so much gloom*
> *And you two sing and dance instead!*

The moon fell silent and shame clouded its face. The bald man mumbled, "Don't shout, the neighbors are sleeping." But Zohar continued to reprimand him for his dishonesty: she already knows that there are no neighbors around. The bald man, now humbled and contrite, begins to apologize: true, there are no neighbors around and he lives there in solitude. When he saw the moon, so big, so round and shiny, he greeted it cheerfully and the two of them had some fun together.

Zohar relents and her anger dissipates. She tells the bald man, "I know you did not mean to hurt anyone; it's nice that you and the moon had some fun together.

> *But without the moon shedding its light*
> *Ships cannot find their way in the night*
> *Jackals have no one to howl at.*
> *Without the moon watching behind the wall*
> *I cannot fall asleep al all.*

The moon was silent, dropped its head
 Zohar could do nothing but wait,
 Then the man opened the cottage door."

The moon climbs the tall ladder, higher and higher, and from the top of the ladder, it whisperingly promises to come visit every month. Thus, the last station marks the end of the quest and the disruption of the horizontal paratactic progression.

The story opens and concludes with an untrustworthy adult: the father who promises Zohar that a big bright moon will shine through her window, which proves false, and a bald man who misinforms Zohar while hiding and hogging the moon. In between, there is an Odyssean quest to find the missing moon.

What, then is the didactic moral offered to the formal readers? Even though adults usually try to shield and protect children, they don't always succeed. You, the child, have to be determined and attuned to your thoughts and feelings, and let them guide you toward your goal.

SLEEPING WITH A MONSTER

The Story "Good Night Monster" by Shira Geffen

Like many children's stories, "Good Night Monster" proceeds along two parallel tracks, one a paratactic continuum where the narrative units are presented consecutively and exhibit a marked similarity, the second an external element that imposes itself on the horizontal sequence to disrupt it and bring about a conclusion.

The parallel track is an Odyssean quest that takes the main protagonist from one station to the next in search of a solution to a problem that besets him or her.

"Good Night Monster" opens with Ruthie, a little girl who goes to sleep every night fearing the dreams that may come. Her mother tells her, "Dreams are imaginary things / When you open your eyes, they melt away." But Ruthie's father realizes that this logical explanation does not pacify the little girl. "He strokes her head / And kisses all her freckles." But Ruthie is still anxious. She tells her parents, "There is a blue monster with orange nose/ As soon as I close my eyes, it enters my dream." Thus, Ruthie's father decides to take action. From the top shelf, he takes down a pink toy, a baby elephant named Yossi, and gives it to his daughter. As soon as Ruthie hugs the pink elephant's trunk, she calms down and falls asleep.

Here we note an aberration from the traditional quest pattern: instead of a character's progression from one station to the next, here other characters, each in its turn, travel from one station to the next. Moreover, at each station we encounter one frightened character and one comforting character. But in each transition, the previously comforting character becomes frightened and longs to find another comforting character and so on.

The units of the horizontal paratactic continuum are identical, and an external element is required to disrupt the sequence.

Thus, Yossi, the pink elephant that has put Ruthie to sleep, now sits in her bed in the dark room, his eyes wide open, and he is gripped with fear and anxiety. He notices a tiny light from a glowworm passing through. Yossi calls out to the glowworm and the latter allays his fears so he can relax and fall asleep. Now it is the glowworm's turn to succumb to fright and anxiety: a black shadow pops up, dancing on the wall constantly changing its shape. In great distress, the glowworm turns to Elisheva the doll. The doll comes over, hugs the frightened glowworm and lulls it to sleep.

But Elisheva the doll is soon gripped by fear herself. "What's moving there behind the curtain?" Elisheva notices a clock hanging on the wall and tries to find solace in its hands. The clock responds willingly and lies down next to the doll, encircling her in its hands.

"The hours disperse all around
The minutes bounce up and down.

Who can tell if this is real time
Or only dream time?

However, the confusion between real time and dream time does not bother the doll, which promptly overcomes her fears and fall asleep.

Now it's the clock's turn. Having allayed the doll's fears, it becomes restless and can't fall asleep. The clock looks around for someone or something to give it instructions how to fall asleep, but all its friends are already fast asleep. Suddenly, the clock hears a hiccup. He spots a blue monster standing, shaking, in the corner of the room.

And here a surprise awaits the reader: The monster that so frightened little Ruthie earlier is itself trembling with fear. The clock is not scared of the monster: it invites the monster to sit in bed next to it. The monster cooperates and gathers the clock to its trembling body. The clock falls asleep, a pleasant smile hovering on its lips. Thus, the scary blue monster that terrorized little Ruthie earlier proves to be a friendly, warm and kindly creature.

Just as everyone else—Little Ruthie, the pink elephant, the glowworm, the doll Elisheva, the clock—can't fall asleep because they are gripped by terror, the blue monster with the orange nose lies in bed trembling with fear. A tear drops from its blue cheek and lands on the palm of Little Ruthie's hand. While still fast asleep, Little Ruthie hugs the Blue Monster. And this is the alien element that disrupts the horizontal paratactic progression and brings the story to its conclusion.

Up to this point, the "metamorphosis" of the characters had one direction: from a soothing figure to a frightened figure. Here, Little Ruthie reverses the direction: from a frightful figure she turns into a soothing figure, thereby bringing the quest to an end: all the characters reach peace and quiet.

The didactic message for the young reader is this: fear is natural; everyone experiences fear, but at the same time, one can be rid of fear, overcome it and attain peace and tranquility.

TENDER IS THE TEAR

The Story: "The Lake of Tears"
by Shira Geffen

The story is a typical Odyssey story. And yet, for the reader, the quest is an enigmatic one. The purpose of the journey is made clear only toward the end of the story. In literary theory, there is a distinction between plot and exposition. Exposition is informative material that precedes the plot: the background to the story, the time and place of the events of the plot, the main characters and their relationships, all these are expository elements that enable the readers to find their way in the plot and to familiarize themselves with the characters at the outset. Thus, the place of the exposition is before the plot along the continuum of the unfolding elements of the story.

However, quite often—as is the case in this story—the exposition is not found in its "traditional, historical" place, but is deferred to a later stage (sometimes much later) along the unfolding plot. Postponing the expositional information creates an information gap. What has taken place before the beginning of the plot? Who are the main characters taking part in the plot? What are the relations and interactions among them? These expositional gaps reflect our curiosity: what happened in the past and precedes the plot? [Other gaps reflect suspense: What is

going to happen? What does the plot have in store for us?]
Expositional gaps of curiosity are crucial for the understanding of the story, its plot and characters. Thus,
expositional gaps warrant a dynamic, accelerated and
vigorous reading process, since a persistent question
hovers over the reading process, demanding to know what
happened before the events described in the story. What
causes the characters to behave in a certain way? What is
behind their interaction with the other characters?

This is what happens in this story. The main protagonist is a tear that drips down a rounded cheek, then hops
on a shoulder, on an arm and down to the floor, then rolls
down the stairs toward the door...and the journey continues. But there is a glaring absence of expositional information: What is the source of the tear? Whose eye generat-
ed the tear? A man? A woman? A boy? A girl? Is it a tear of
joy or of sorrow? All these details are hidden from the
reader (to be supplied later). This prods the reader to
adopt an "ambitious" reading process; the reader is
impelled to apply energy and resolve in order to figure out
what happens.

Moreover, the tear that has started the Odyssean quest
passively gradually becomes active, motivated and full of
initiative. In the meantime, the future-oriented suspense
gap still hovers over the story: What is the purpose of the
quest? What is the tear trying to achieve? Where is it
going? Here, too, the expository information will be revealed only at the end of the reading process. Again, this
gives rise to a dynamic, vibrant reading process driven by
the reader's desire to know and understand.

The next stage in the tear's Odyssey is the following:

The tear clung to a running cat's whisker
A gust of wind tore it away
It flew and landed on a unicycle.

Here, we note a change in the tear's trajectory: it is no longer passive; it is becoming active and takes initiatives:

There came a clown with a painted smile
Who looked happy even when he was sad.
He hopped on the unicycle saddle
The tear was underneath
Clinging to the cycle.

The tear exhibits tenacity and determination in clinging to a unicycle in motion.

The tear revolved inside the cycle
The entire world was reflected in it
And so the tear felt that it was the world.'

The activism and initiative that fill the tear now infuse it with self-aggrandizement and arrogance, reminiscent of Biblical Joseph who, in his dreams, imagined that he was the center of the world.

Although she got giddy
Confusing earth and sky,

The tear still remembered
where it was streaming.

Here the narrative begins to fill the suspension gap in the plot that is directed toward the future. Where is the tear heading? What are the purpose and the goal of its odyssey?

Next, the tear continues her energetic, activist pursuit and jumps on a wooden scarecrow. The tear asks the scarecrow, "Do you know how to get to the Great Lake of Tears?" So this is the destination of the journey, this is the purpose of the odyssey. The scarecrow tells the tear: Because of global warming, the Lake of Tears is not as big as it used to be. Still, he encourages the tear to continue her pursuit. "Don't lose heart," he tells her. The scarecrow blew on the tear and pushed it to the ground. Here the tear's journey takes a turn:

> *It's nice to be outside,' thought the tear*
> *As she grew heavier and heavier*
> *From all the grains of sand she has absorbed*
> > *on the way,*
> *And from the dry leaves*
> *And the upside-down umbrellas of the*
> > *groundsels.*

The tear continues her quest with determination and verve,

She cleared paths that never existed before
For other tears that may come after,
For there are no signposts and no maps leading
to the Lake of Tears.

The tear now is not just active and enterprising; it evinces initiative, savvy and leadership.

Eventually, the tear reaches a steep cliff and stops. The cliff overlooks the Lake of Tears. It is smaller than she imagined, but supremely beautiful. However, the distance and the height scare the tear and she is too fearful to drop down to the lake.

To her surprise, she notices another tear standing nearby. The two tears ask the same question simultaneously, "Where did you drop from?" And here the information gap begins to be filled; the expositional information that was deferred earlier (prompting curiosity about the antecedent plot) is offered to the reader: the tear set on her journey after dropping from the blue eye of a little boy who had found out that his goldfish had died. His mother tried her best to console him; she bought him eight new goldfish and two silverfish. The child managed to stem the flow of tears, but one tear escaped and dropped from his eye.

The tear that just joined the traveling tear reports that it had dropped from the brown eye of an old woman whose granddaughter hugged her and whispered, "You are the sweetest grandma in the world."

Thus, a tear born of sorrow joins a tear born of joy. The two tears draw courage and determination from the emotional partnership they have just formed, and together they roll down from the cliff toward the Lake of Tears, which shimmers magnificently when the sun bathes in it and lights it from within. "The tears looked at each and knew that it was time."

At that moment, the two tears dropped into the lake, mixed together and became froth; now there was no way of knowing which one was born of sorrow and which one was born of joy.

In fact, the ending of the story is two endings that contradict each other. On the one hand, the ending is optimistic: it sends a message of unity and harmony. On the other, the ending is pessimistic: it sends a desperate message of loss of identity and individuality. Since the story is aimed at very young children (presumably not older than five), the adult reading the story to the child will prefer the optimistic ending and play down the pessimistic one.

RE-WRITING THE BIBLE

The Story "Noah"
by Yoram Taharlev

The story "Noah" demonstrates the dual purposes that a children's author has when retelling Biblical stories. On the one hand, there is a wish to introduce the young target audience to the richness of the Bible stories, and on the other hand there is an attempt to "protect" the young audience by eliminating from the story those unsavory elements that contain evil and ugliness that are inherent in the original Biblical story. Equally slated for excision from children's stories are sexual references. This is the case of Noah's story that centers round the flood.

The background to the Biblical story of the flood is the following:

> *These are the generations of Noah: Noah was a just man, and perfect in his generation, and Noah walked with God. And Noah begat three sons, Shem, Ham, and Japheth. The earth also was corrupt before God, and the earth was filled with violence. And God looked upon the earth, and behold, it was corrupt: for all flesh had corrupted his way upon the earth. And God said unto Noah, The end of all flesh is come before*

me, for the earth is filled with violence through them. And behold, I will destroy them with the earth. Make thee an ark of gopher wood; rooms shalt thou make in the ark, and shalt pitch it within and without with pitch. And this is the fashion which thou shalt make it of..." (Genesis 6, 9-16)

There comes a detailed description of the construction of the ark, the animals it will house, and a reiteration of the reason and purpose of the flood, which is to destroy all God's creatures (the Bible does not address the question of what the animals' guilt and why they, too, are doomed).

The story of the flood exists in many mythological texts that preceded the Bible, such as the Sumerian Flood story (2100 BCE), the Babylonian Flood story, whose protagonist is Gilgamesh (1800 BCE), as well as the Finnish Flood story ("Kelavala"), Hindu mythology, and others. In all these stories there is a flood and the protagonist is enjoined to build an ark.

In the story, Noah is described as a pleasant, pious craftsman. He is always in good humor, singing while he works. Thus, the pious Noah—about whom the Bible gives no other description—undergoes a dramatic transformation when he is transferred to a children's story. He becomes a graceful grandfatherly figure, a hardworking carpenter who never stops singing while he works.

One day, Noah gets up, stretches his limbs, and announces that God has revealed to him that He is about to bring a flood upon the earth. It is now incumbent on

Noah to build a large ark. There is no mention of a reason for the flood, not a hint of the destructive, cataclysmic nature of the flood.

When the construction of the ark is complete, the animals are invited to board it. In the Bible the animals are housed in the ark in order to preserve their species after the flood. In our story no reason is given for the preservation of the animals, only the fact that the animals contribute to the merry carnival atmosphere on the ark. Any mention of the preservation of the species would imply the original destruction of all God's creatures, something that does not accord well with a story aimed at children.

This is how the flood is described in the story:

> *Rain, rain, rain and wind,*
> *Wind, wind, wind and rain,*
> *No window is open,*
> *An abandoned door bangs.*
> *Water, water, water, water,*
> *The streets fill with water,*
> *The houses fill with water,*
> *The fields fill with water,*
> *The roofs submerge in the water,*
> *The trees are drowned.*
> *The mountains drown,*
> *The entire world*
> *Disappears under water..."*

The flood is described in accordance (albeit partial) with the original story, but not a word about destruction,

death, punishment and retribution. Compare this to the
Biblical story:

> *And the waters prevailed, and were increased*
> *greatly upon the earth; and the ark went under*
> *the face of the waters. And the water prevailed*
> *exceedingly upon the earth... And all flesh died*
> *that moved upon the earth, both of fowl, and of*
> *cattle, and of beast, and of every creeping thing*
> *that creepeth upon the earth, and every man. All*
> *in whose nostrils was the breath of life, of all*
> *that was on the dry land died. And every living*
> *substance was destroyed which was upon the*
> *face of the ground, both man, and cattle and the*
> *creeping things and the fowl of the heaven; and*
> *they were destroyed from the earth; and Noah*
> *only remained alive and they that were with him*
> *in the ark.* (Genesis 7, 17-24)

In the story "Noah," however, while the entire world is
covered in water:

> *While a storm is raging outside,*
> *Inside a song is heard,*
> *Noah sits by the fireplace*
> *Rubbing his hands,*
> *Warming his feet,*
> *Singing a nameless song,*
> *Yabba-babba-babba,*
> *God will prevail!"*

In the Bible, Noah first sends a raven to check "if the waters were abated" but the raven came back to the ark. Noah then sends a dove, but the dove, too, finding no rest for her feet, comes back. Seven days later, Noah sends the dove again, and this time she comes back with an olive branch in her beak. When he sends her a third time, the dove does not return because the water had receded and the land is dry.

However, in the children's story, only a dove is sent forth, not a raven, because the black raven, with its negative connotations, is deemed unfit to be included in a story for children.

Thus, even though the story "Noah" is based on the Biblical text, the Genesis story is only a starting point from which to create an independent text better suited for young audiences.

The story is a "flood light" story, devoid of the original morbid, gloomy, anxiety- inducing connotations; only a fraction of the original plot remains in this version for young readers.

Two Stories that Amos Oz's Mother, Fania Mussman Klauzner, Told Her Son When He Was Young
[Retold by the adult Amos Oz]

In our house, three wicker stools stood around the kitchen table that was covered with a floral oilcloth. The kitchen itself was narrow, low slung and dark; the floor had sunk a little, the walls were covered with soot from the Primus stove and the kerosene burner; the sole window looked out on a basement courtyard surrounded by gray concrete walls.

Sometimes, after my father had gone off to work, I would come into the kitchen, sit on his stool so I could face my mother and listen to her tell stories while peeling and slicing vegetables or sorting lentils, picking out the black ones and setting them aside on a plate. Later, I would feed those black lentils to the birds in the yard.

My mother's stories were strange, unlike any of the children's stories that were told in other homes in those days, and unlike the stories that I later told to my own children; her stories were shrouded in haze: they had no beginning and no end and seemed to have emerged from a thicket, revealed themselves for a brief moment, evoking weird sensations and anxiety; they wiggled in front of me like twisted shadows on the wall, fascinating me, sometimes sending shivers down my spine, and then they retreated to the thick woods before I could figure out what had happened. To this day, I remember some of my mother's stories almost verbatim; for instance, the story about Alliluyev, the hoary old man.

Over the high mountains, beyond the deep rivers and the desolate steppes, there was a remote little village of ramshackle cottages. At the edge of the village, near a forest of black fir trees, lived a poor, blind, mute old man, who had no friend or relative in the world, and his name was Alliluyev.

Old man Alliluyev was more ancient than any man living in the village, or in the valley or in the prairie. He was not just old, he was ancient, primordial. He was so antiquated that his bent back had sprouted moss. Instead of hair, black mushrooms grew on his head, and from his hollow cheeks burgeoned hyssop and lichen. Gnarly brown roots grew out of his feet and in the sockets of his sightless eyes, shiny glowworms settled.

Old Alliluyev was older than the forest, older than the snow, even older than Time itself. One day a rumor spread in the village that in the depth of his cottage—whose windows had never been opened—dwelt another old man, Chernichortin, who was much older, blinder, muter

*and poorer than Alliluyev, and who was also
deaf and paralyzed and obliterated like an old
Tartar coin.*

*On snowy nights the villagers recounted that old
Alliluyev was secretly taking care of Chernichortin, washing him and cleaning his sores,
setting the table for him and putting him to sleep,
feeding him berries and giving him well water or
melted snow to drink. Sometimes, at night, he
would sing him lullabies, "Liu-liu-liu, have no
fear, my treasure, liu-liu-liu, don't shiver, my
precious."*

*And the two of them would fall asleep hugging
each other, the old man and his older man. And
outside, there was only wind and snow. If the
wolves have not devoured them, then they are
still living there together in the tumbledown
cottage. The wolf howls in the forest and the
wind roars in the chimney.*

There were old people in our neighborhood in Amos Street
in Jerusalem, but their slow, painful shuffle, as they
passed by our house was nothing but a pale, faded,
clumsy copy of the frightening, spine-tingling reality of old
man Alliluyev, the ancient, hoary, primeval character from
my mother's stories, just as Tel Arza Copse was nothing
more than a crude amateurish sketch of the thick primordial forests of my mother's stories. The lentils my mother

cooked were a disappointing substitute for the mushrooms and forest bushes, blueberries, blackberries and gooseberries that populated her stories. Reality itself was but a failed attempt, a flat and bootless effort to replicate the rich world that her words had created.

Here is a story my mother told me about a women and blacksmiths. She did not choose her words and did not take into account my tender age when she exposed me to the expanses of the distant and picturesque provinces of the language. Few children had ever set foot in those regions, where linguistic birds-of-paradise resided:

> Many years ago, in a peaceful village in the land of Enolaria, in the district of the Innermost Valleys, there lived three brothers, three blacksmiths, Misha, Alyosha and Antosha. They were robust, hirsute, bearlike men. All winter long they slept, and in summer they fashioned plowshares, shoed horses, sharpened knives, pounded daggers, forged blades and melted old shafts.

> One day, Misha, the eldest, went to the nearby district of Troshiban. He was gone for many days, and when he returned, he was not alone; he brought with him a laughing girlish woman named Tatiana, Tanya, Tanichka. She was the most beautiful woman ever seen in the whole land of Enolaria. Misha's younger brothers ground their teeth and kept quiet all day. When-

*ever either of them looked at her, Tanichka
would laugh her pealing laugh until the man was
forced to lower his eyes. And if she looked at one
of them, the brother she had chosen trembled
and averted his eyes. The cottage where the
brothers lived had only one small room and in
that single room lived Misha and Tanichka and
the furnace and the anvils and the wild brother
Alyosha and the silent brother Antosha, among
heavy iron hammers and axes and chisels and
rods, chains and metal sheets.*

*And so it happens that one day Misha was
pushed into the furnace, and Alyosha took
Tanichka for himself. For seven weeks, the lovely
Tanichka was the wife of wild Alyosha, until a
heavy hammer fell on him and crushed his chest.*

*Antosha, the silent one, buried his brother and
took his place. Seven weeks later, while the two
were eating mushroom pie, Antosha suddenly
turned pale, then blue and then he choked to
death. From that day on, young itinerant blacksmiths from all over Enolaria came and stayed in
the cottage, but none ever dared stay there for
more than seven weeks. One would stay for a
week, another for two nights.*

*And Tanya? All the blacksmiths of Enolaria
know that Tanichka loves blacksmiths who come
for a week, for two or three days, for overnight;*

half-naked they toil in the smithy, hammering,
forging, shoeing horses, but she has no patience
for a visitor who forgets to get up and leave. Two
or three weeks are enough, but seven weeks?
That wouldn't do.

ANALYSIS OF THE TWO STORIES BY AMOS OZ'S MOTHER

These are not conventional children's stories. First, the mother never wrote them down. Second, as the grown-up Amos Oz himself notes, these are strange stories, without distinct beginning or ending. They are not suitable for young audiences because of the gothic elements they contain and the wintry, European landscapes they evoke.

The first story contains two old characters, Alliluyev and Chernichortin, but these characters are completely static; there is no plot and no progression whatsoever. The fact that the two characters are analogous prevents any plot development. The only hint of a possible plot relies on the description of how one old man takes care of the other. Thus, the story can, perhaps, be described as a story of atmosphere, or mood. The atmosphere is dark, heavy, wintry, European and Gothic.

Two errors are found in the story. We are told that old man Alliluyev sings lullabies to the older man Chernichortin. But we are also told that Alliluyev is mute, and that Chernichortin is deaf. Still, these errors do not dispel or detract from the intriguing Gothic quality of the tale.

The second story, about the three blacksmiths and the pretty Tatiana is based on the familiar literary motif of *'la belle dame sans merci'*—the cruel, fair lady.

(Cf. John Keats' ballad by that name. Keats' ballad (1820) in turn was inspired by a much earlier ballad by Alan Chartier (1424).

The beautiful heartless lady is an attractive but lethal woman. She lures men, then spurns and humiliates them, often causing their death. This is the motif at the center of the second story. It opens with three robust, hairy brothers, three blacksmiths named Misha, Alyosha, and Antosha. They hibernate through the winter, and only in summer do they ply their trade industriously, forging plowshares, shoeing horses, hammering daggers, honing blades, and melting old metal poles.

One day, the eldest brother Misha goes to a nearby district and stays there for many days. When he comes back he brings back a beautiful, cheerful, young woman, Tanya. Misha's brothers are consumed with envy. The girl has a pealing laughter that makes the envious brothers lower their gaze.

One day Misha is pushed into the melting furnace and Alyosha takes Tanya to himself. In the context of the story, it is assumed that the envious Alyosha is the one who pushed Misha into the furnace so he could take possession of Tanya. But soon it is Alyosha's turn. One day a hammer falls on him and crushes his chest.

Antosha, the youngest brother, takes possession of Tanya. Here, too, it is assumed that the envious Antosha murdered his brother so he could possess the woman. There are echoes here of the Biblical story of Abel and Cain.

But here a surprise awaits the reader: seven weeks later, while Antosha and Tanya dine on a mushroom pie, "Antosha turned pale, then blue, then choked to death."

Since there was no brother left to kill Antosha, and since Antosha and Tanya lived by themselves in the cottage, and since we assume that Tanya baked the pie, the only logical explanation is that it was Tanya who poisoned Antosha.

Later, we are told that soon after Antosha's death, young blacksmiths from all over the region came to the cottage, and as long as their stay did not exceed a week or two, Tanya welcomed them with open arms. The last sentence in the story expresses her intention: "she has no patience for a visitor who forgets to get up and leave. Two or three weeks are enough, but seven weeks? That wouldn't do." She likes young blacksmiths who come for a couple of days, working in the smithy, hammering and forging but never staying longer than a week or two—and seven weeks are out of the question.

Now the true meaning of the story is revealed, and all the pieces of the puzzle fall into place. Tanya cannot abide any blacksmith staying with her for more than seven weeks. Antosha, the youngest brother who lived with her for seven weeks, died after eating a poisoned mushroom pie she had baked for him (she must have known which part of the pie did not contain the poison). Antosha had no brothers left who could murder him out of jealousy.

Since both older brothers had spent lengthy periods of time with Tanya, it was she who did them in. Misha was pushed into the furnace, and Alyosha was crushed by a hammer. Thus, the Cain-Abel hypothesis of lethal envy is proved wrong; it must be replaced by the *Belle Dame Sans Merci* paradigm. The reading and the interpretation of the story are turned on their head and acquire a new meaning.

In this story, too, the bleak, wintry European atmosphere determines the character of the story. Moreover, the heavy sexual context (so blatantly conveyed by the sensuous Tanya, the thickset hairy brothers and the half naked young blacksmiths, the object of the woman's lascivious looks) joins the dreary, Gothic atmosphere to create a unique ambience that generates fear and lust.

Those were the stories that Fania Mussman-Klauzner told to her son, Amos Oz. It is hard to recommend these stories for young readers. And yet, those were the stories Oz heard in his childhood, and he remembered them, almost word for word, seventy years later.

EPILOGUE

The chapters of this book seem to indicate that children's literature can be analyzed with the same interpretive tools used for any other kind of literature. At the same time, these chapters seek to temper the enthusiasm of certain scholars of children's literature who claim that there is no difference at all between children's and adult literature.

Even though children's literature can be analyzed with the same tools used for adult literature, the following observations are valid and indisputable: the plot in children's literature is comparatively scant and simplistic, the characters flat and one-dimensional, and the vocabulary relatively limited.

These strictures befit texts that are aimed at children; the target audience dictates its nature. But the claim that there is no difference between children's literature and adult literature is baseless. In most stories and poems for children (though not in all of them), one can find a moral, a didactic lesson to be drawn from the text. The moral can be either plain and obvious or concealed and veiled, requiring adult "intervention" by the unofficial reader of the text in order to expose and elucidate the didactic message.

One thing is clear: despite the generic limitations of children's literature, it has potential to be valuable and meritorious.

ABOUT THE AUTHOR

Dr. Yair Mazor is a professor of modern Hebrew literature and biblical literature with the University of Wisconsin–Milwaukee. Professor Mazor is the author of 28 books and over 250 articles and critical reviews. Dr. Mazor's fields of study are modern Hebrew literature, Enlightenment Hebrew literature in the 19th centuries in Eastern Europe, biblical literature, comparative literature, Scandinavian literature, and Hebrew children's literature.

Dr. Mazor has earned numerous scholarly awards, among them the Shpam Prize and Dov Sadan Prize from the University of Tel Aviv for two of his books; the Baron Prize for exceptional excellence in research in the field of Jewish Studies; the "Distinguished Undergraduate Teaching Award" from the University of Wisconsin–Milwaukee; and a national award, the "Most Distinguished Scholar of Hebrew Studies in the USA, the Friedman Prize.

www.ingramcontent.com/pod-product-compliance
Lightning Source LLC
Chambersburg PA
CBHW060433090426
42733CB00011B/2264